*The University
and the
Counterculture*

The University and the Counterculture

Inaugural and Other Addresses
by Edward J. Bloustein

RUTGERS UNIVERSITY PRESS
New Brunswick   *New Jersey*

780104

Library of Congress Cataloging in Publication Data

Bloustein, Edward J
  The university and the counterculture.

  1. Education, Higher—1965–   —Addresses, essays,
lectures. 2. College students—Addresses, essays,
lectures. I. Title.
LB2325.B56   378′.008   72–2583
ISBN 0–8135–0733–2 Cloth
ISBN 0–8135–0744–8 Paper

In a slightly different form, "The New Student" was first published in *Liberal Education*, October 1968, and "A New Academic
Social Contract," in the same magazine for March 1970. Also in a
slightly different form, "Parents of the Counterculture" first appeared
in *Hadassah Magazine*, October 1971.

Contents

Part I
The Nature of the Contemporary University

Where Reason Resides

WE GATHER HERE TODAY to celebrate and bear witness to the continuity of purpose of that community of scholarship and learning we call Rutgers, the State University. In accepting office as its seventeenth president, I pledge to serve it truly and well.

It was not too long ago that accepting the presidency of a great and distinguished university was the occasion of joy and honor, pure and simple. Today the same act is regarded by many as an act of foolhardiness, and by others who are more charitable as an act of courage; there is nothing pure and simple about it at all.

The changed social perception of the university presidency is symptomatic of the uncertainty of purpose and the failure of nerve of the contemporary university. We are filled with misgivings concerning

Inaugural Address delivered on November 10, 1971, in the Rutgers University Gymnasium, New Brunswick, New Jersey.

the goals and methods of higher education, concerning its governance, concerning its student body and concerning its relationship to society at large. And, in each instance, our doubts are pervasive and debilitating. We even seem to lack confidence in our own capacity to resolve them.

I speak today about the nature and goals of the university. Why do we gather together in academic communities? My answer will seem too simple to many of you. But I believe that in periods of social and personal distress we tend to lose sight of first principles and sometimes a restatement of them restores perspective and equanimity.

The university is the place where reason resides. It is, in fact, the institutionalization of reason. To be sure, men and women in government and business, and in shops and hospitals, undertake to think rationally about the issues before them. They explore alternative possibilities, examine the past for insight into what to expect in the future, attempt to put emotion and bias to one side and in other ways apply systematic thought to the issues at hand. But in a medical office the aim is to cure the sick, in a court of law it is to adjudge liability under the law and in a factory to produce a product at a profit. Reason is enlisted in each of these enterprises, but none of them embody it in the sense in which the university does. For in the university, reason is the very goal rather than the mere instrument of the enterprise.

The university exists to reason; reason is the very purpose of its being.

It is by now a commonplace of contemporary educational philosophy that this purpose is fulfilled by three different kinds of activity, the discovery of ideas, their transmission from generation to generation and their application to the problems of our society. Research, teaching and service to the community comprise the work product of the university.

The malaise of the contemporary university resides in some large measure in the fact that it has not yet achieved a harmonious ordering of the three tasks it has undertaken. My thesis is that we can only achieve true cohesion of function by examining each of our tasks in the light of the first principle of our existence, reason. Seen in the light of that first principle, teaching, research and service to society are complementary functions, each reinforcing the other. But if teaching, or research or service to the community assumes a life of its own, if any one of them loses sight of its common root, the consequence is discord in the university community and a limitation on its capacity to fulfill successfully any one of its undertakings.

Let us look at each of the three great roles of the university in turn. Teaching or the transmission of knowledge is at the very heart of what the university is all about. Three questions associated with teaching are the cause of contemporary concern. What shall we teach? How shall we teach it? And for what purposes shall we teach it?

In an earlier day, there was a relatively limited system of knowledge; the roles educated men took in society were much less differentiated; the problems of our society were much simpler; and knowledge played a less significant part in the conduct of our life. In this earlier period teaching and learning were indeed uncomplicated phenomena. However, in our day the social function learning performs has become more important and more complex, and continued study has yielded a vastly complicated and enormous body of knowledge. As a consequence, teachers have become more specialized and the training students require to assume responsibility in our complex society has become increasingly varied. In other words, the increasing sophistication of knowledge and the extraordinary demands we make on it have imposed a severe strain on the teaching function of the university. The university can no longer pretend—if ever it could—to teach all there is to know. The trend towards specialization of subject matter has in turn led to competing claims to primacy in the undergraduate curriculum and to controversy over what courses shall be required in our curriculum.

As I view the matter, however, our purpose is not to teach subject matter but to teach the modes of human reason. We must help our students discover how to come to know something, what it means to know something and how one goes about knowing it. The object in undergraduate education is not to teach a variety of subjects, but to teach a variety of ways of knowing. In an age of greatly specialized learning, in a time when the range of knowledge is vast and the uses to which our community puts our learning is constantly subject to change, all we can hope to teach is how to know, how to cope with ignorance.

I do not mean to suggest that we can teach the ways of knowing without teaching some subject matter, without studying specific problems. Nor do I mean that we should teach courses which survey general fields of knowledge. I rather mean that in teaching specialized fields of study, our object should be to teach method, to inculcate the ways of knowing. Reason, as our first principle, should serve as our guide to harmonizing the competing demands of specialized subject matter.

What to teach is one problem; how to teach is another. Traditional attitudes towards teaching are currently under attack and rightly so. Book learning and learning by rote simply do not serve the purpose of inculcating the discipline of reason. The student must become a doer and learn by experience. Learning must become a form of apprenticeship, and apprenticeship to the teacher skilled in the ways of knowing. And skill in the ways of knowing can only be achieved by practicing those ways through independent research, experiment and experience in applying knowledge to problems of the real world.

It is a mistake, however, to glorify experience and field work as educational ends in themselves. Experience which is blind to theory and ideas, field work which is untested by the discipline of intellectual criticism—these are barren exercises in educational terms, however satisfying they may be otherwise. Experience is, of course, a great teacher, but having an experience is not the same thing as knowing something about the experience or understanding it. Experience is a more effective tool of understanding if it is undertaken to test an idea. Practice or field work is of most significant educational value when it serves reason, is conducted within a scientific and conceptual perspective, provides intellectual insight and develops intellectual disciplines.

The last of the concerns about the teaching mission of the university which I shall touch upon is the purpose we serve in teaching. We train young men and women to serve society in a great variety of ways: as community workers, as teachers and scientists, as lawyers and librarians. One full measure of our service to the community is in preparing educated men and women to serve its needs. Thus, in performing our teaching mission, we are also fulfilling our public service mission.

But here we enter upon what seems like a paradox. For it turns out that the best preparation for a vocation or profession is no preparation at all. What I mean by this is that the student who prepares specifically and narrowly for some vocation or profession is inadequately prepared, while the student who is absorbed with learning how to learn, the student attracted to the broad reaches of theory and knowledge, is best prepared to cope with the demands of a vocation or profession. The basis of the paradox is this. Those who serve a vocation or profession well are those who practice it creatively, those who can solve novel problems, lead their field in new directions and meet new challenges. These are the men and women whose grasp of the ways of reason and theory give them a capacity to go beyond the rote and repetitive demands of their calling to see new horizons and approach new problems. Professional and vocational stagnation can only be avoided by those students who are trained in research method and theory.

Breadth of undergraduate and graduate training has another virtue: it prepares young men and women not only to practice their vocations and professions well, but also to use the ways of reason in fashioning their individual lives and the life of their society. The educated man or woman brings the perspective of history and culture into social life. Such a student helps the society reach beyond technology, beyond the mechanics of professional and vocational skills, to the ethical and aesthetic horizons of human existence. Education at its best prepares us to put skills and techniques to new purposes; it prepares us to examine critically the quality and not merely the mechanics of life.

In sum, the university teaches its students to serve their community with a great variety of skills, but this service is enriched by a common attachment to the university's climate of research and theory. The touchstone is once again found in the modes and ways of reason.

Having completed this brief survey of the problems associated with teaching, I turn to examine the two other university tasks I spoke of earlier, research and service to the community. Research capacity is of the very essence of the university system. It provides the intellectual capital on which teaching and service to society prosper. The men and women of our faculty are dedicated to exploring and enlarging the ranges of human knowledge. In laboratories, libraries, studios and offices, they seek out answers to the intellectual puzzles of nature. They grasp for theories and systems of belief which will help us understand and control the world in which we live.

Once again we encounter what seems like a paradox. The more disinterested, pure and removed research is, the more productive and relevant it often turns out to be. Men and women tied down to serve immediate practical needs frequently suffer from limitations of intellectual vision enforced by the pressures of time and the need for an immediate result. While those intellectual workers who are blessed one way or another to roam freely where their curiosity and passion for truth take them produce the most fruitful ideas and theories. The research worker in the university serves its purposes by continually enriching the body of knowledge to be taught to its students and to be put by them and others to the service of the community. Seen in this perspective, research is a partner in the common enterprise of the university rather than an independent operation with a life of its own.

What has caused concern about the role of research in the university in recent years is that, in some instances, it has begun to serve purposes extraneous to the university. Researchers under contract to the government and private corporations have begun to become private entrepreneurs, serving the needs and working at a pace and in a fashion dictated by those who pay their contract costs. Such research has become too result-oriented to serve the purposes of scholarship and science. And the men and women involved in it have become too detached from the teaching mission and the life of the university.

The resolution of this problem cannot consist in forbidding research contracts, nor can it consist in requiring all research workers to teach. Both of these alternatives are simplistic solutions to a complex problem. The fact is that contract research directed to the solution of a great variety of governmental, community, agricultural and industrial problems is a necessary element of the service a university must provide, and it is also the necessary testing ground of the theoretical work researchers do. Moreover, the fact is that researchers can also be effective academic colleagues even when they do not teach in the classroom, as long as what they do and how they do it provides a model and a form of inspiration and stimulation to teaching colleagues and students. The solution of our difficulty in respect of contract research is not to forbid it, but rather to harness it by insisting that it be held accountable by the university to nurture reason. Contract research can and should take place in the university, but only insofar as it continues to serve the university's purposes as determined by the university itself and not by the contract researcher or his paymaster.

Service to the community is the last of the three great tasks the university undertakes. It does so when it teaches its students to assume the place of educated men and women working in a variety of vocations and professions. The university best serves society by staffing its offices with young men and women who bring reason, sensibility and skill to bear on its problems and purposes.

Likewise, the university serves society by fostering pure and applied research. In government, factory and farm, in homes and in courts of law, the research product of the university provides the intellectual capital necessary for growth and development. Rationality and its products constitute the tools and the methods to be used by the community in meeting its needs.

The contemporary university is threatened with losing its soul, not because it serves society, but because for too long it has served too narrow a range of social interests. The paymasters of government and industry have distorted the life of the university by luring too much of its intellectual capital into enterprises of war, barren technology and commercialism. The university cannot and should not forbid defense research, any more than it should forbid any other research; to do so would run contrary to the freedom associated with the life of reason. But the university can and should see that external paymasters do not, by dint of lucrative contracts, determine the university's research priorities. The profit and affluence associated with certain research should not skew the university's own system of reward and status. The university should positively foster research which may not be profitable at all and which may, in fact, have no market or application at all.

This obligation to see that intellectual talent is put to the service of unpopular and uncommercial social interests does not arise out of social conscience; the university is and should remain ethically neutral, pursuing no social or political purposes of its own. The obligation to foster research with no application or with applications of little or no profit flows from the life of reason itself. In the scales of reason, profitability and popularity of research make no mark. The only test is the test of truth. And the university must support the search for truth, whether there be profitable application or not.

It should be noted, however, that, all other things being equal, the university should and does favor the application of knowledge to social purpose. Among other reasons, such application is, in some sense, a test of truth. Even where it is not, it is a source of intellectual stimulation, a spur to curiosity and creative awakenings.

I conclude as I began by stating that the life of reason is what brings us together in the university. As such, it serves to harmonize and order the variety of the university's pursuits. For some thirty years, as a student and teacher of philosophy and law and as a college administrator, I have pursued the path of reason. I come to Rutgers to continue that pursuit. Give me your faith, imagination, energy and intelligence and we shall together revive confidence in the house of reason.

A Great University in the
Service of a Great State

THE PRIVILEGE which you have afforded me as president of your state university to address you today is unique. No previous president of this state university or, as far as I have been able to determine, of any other state university, has had such an opportunity before this day. The unique character of this occasion bespeaks some very significant truths about the nature of the state university. The first of these is that the university and the state system of higher education of which it is a part are more important to contemporary society and to this state than they have ever been in the past. If this nation and this state are to meet successfully the awesome challenges presented in our day, it will only be as a result of

Address delivered on November 15, 1971, before a joint session of the New Jersey Legislature, The State House, Trenton, New Jersey.

marshalling the resources of the university and the
other elements of the higher education system. It
portends well for our future that our governor and
our legislative leaders have recognized this fact in
inviting me here today.

The second vital principle symbolized by my pres-
ence here today is that the state university is accountable to the executive and legislative officers of the
state for fulfilling its mission of service to the people
of the state. Although, as a university, we must be
assured the fullest freedom of inquiry and the widest
possible discretion in management, we are responsible to you and the people of the state for the goals
we seek. Freedom as to means and accountability as
to ends should be the rule of our relationship.

The third notable fact which my appearance before this joint session of the legislature evidences is
a new era in the relationship between the state and
its university. From its earliest days as a colonial college to most recent times, Rutgers and the state have
lived with one another, for the most part, on uneasy
terms. On the one hand, the state has not been quite
sure it wanted or could afford a state university. On
the other hand, the university, whether out of conceit about its origins or fear of encroachment on its
academic prerogatives, has also been a reluctant partner in the task of public education.

I come to you today to say that the days of doubt
are over. This great state requires and deserves a

great state university, and we in the university are pleased and proud to serve the people of this state. As I said in my inaugural address last Wednesday the three primary ways the university serves the state are to train its sons and daughters to assume roles of community responsibility, to provide intellectual capital for the community's development, and to undertake directly to fashion solutions to community problems.

Last week I discussed these three tasks from the perspective of the university. Today I would like to discuss them from the perspective of the community to be served. Before turning to these three facets of the university's service, however, let me speak to a circumstance which underlies each of them. New Jersey is the most densely populated state in the nation and one of the most densely populated areas in the world. We are one of the world's great megalopolises. And the state university must reflect this fact.

This means we must educate a new kind of student body—the children of the great centers of urban and suburban life. It means as well that we must develop new intellectual resources, which are required to solve problems generated by the economy, ecology and sociology of the megalopolis. And it means, finally, that we must apply our intellectual resources to the conditions of the cities and the suburbs.

All of this is relatively new to the life of this or any other university. Until recently our colleges and universities educated the children of the middle and upper classes for social and economic leadership or a limited number of professions. The body of knowledge nurtured in the university bore little or no relationship to the social life of the community, and the limited service which was undertaken by the university was service to the farm community. The advent of advanced technology and its application to industry, agriculture and social organization has transformed the conditions of our life and led to the urbanization of our state and nation. And now the university must respond to that urbanization by changing its fundamental character. It must learn how to serve the cities and suburbs of this day as effectively as it served the farms of yesteryear.

This does not mean we can overlook the agricultural community of New Jersey; we are, after all, the Garden State. The products of our fields, fisheries and orchards are still very important to our economy and our people, as is the work of the food processing and distribution industry. The university must continue to serve this segment of the community. But the fact remains that the great majority of our population live and work in urban and suburban centers of the state, and the life of the state is dominated by its megalopolitan character.

Let me now turn to deal with each of the ways the university can serve New Jersey. First, we must train an ever larger number of its sons and daughters for the very wide range of vocations and professions required by the new conditions of our economy and society. Until recently the Black and Puerto Rican minority of the state, found mostly in its urban centers, was unjustly deprived of university education. In the last three or four years we have begun to redress this wrong. Although the program was necessarily undertaken with haste, on balance, I assure you it has been most successful.

We must be able to add more minority faculty members and minority counselors to increase the value of this program. Moreover, we should assure these minority students of adequate financial assistance. To do less than this is to turn the open door of the university into a revolving door.

As important as any of our other admissions problems is that posed by the lower middle class white children of the cities and suburbs. They lack the financial resources to go to private universities, while public universities outside the state are refusing to admit them because of the pressure of their own in-state enrollments. The only way to meet this problem is to provide more educational places in the state university and other institutions of higher education in New Jersey.

Another group of students of the megalopolis whose new needs must be met in the university is women. The conditions of urban and suburban life have created a new consciousness among women.

Many more of them than ever before seek education of the same character and quality as that available to men and seek to enter the same vocations and professions men do. The possibility of their doing so rests on the university's providing flexibility of programming and courses directed to strengthening women's own consciousness of their right to equal status, and providing day-care nurseries for the children of married women who want to continue their education.

The final group of new students of the megalopolis is the older student. The traditional university proceeded on the theory that each of us is to be given but one chance at an education and that that chance occurred between eighteen and twenty-two years of age. The fast-changing character of technology and science, the new leisure, the very advance of knowledge itself, have made the one-chance theory of higher education an anachronism. New ways of educating adults in the university should be found and many more adults than before should be brought into the university.

Enrolling these new students presents formidable problems, of course. It would be useless and wasteful to enroll them at the sacrifice of the quality of the university's current educational program. The very reason these new students want to enter the university is because of its educational excellence. If that is lost in enrolling them, we will not have served their purposes and we will also have wasted the asset we already have on hand. To serve the needs of these new students adequately we will not only have to maintain the quality of our educational program, we will also have to provide new facilities. The recently approved bond issue will allow us some further expansion of educational buildings. We also require, as I previously indicated, day-care centers, and then if we are really to serve our commuters we require more parking and other auxiliary facilities, especially on our commuting campuses in Camden and Newark.

"Why should we meet the needs of these new students?" you may ask. The answer is simple. The children of the cities and suburbs as well as their parents are your constituents and their educational needs are more urgent than most others they face. Moreover, meeting these needs for education is not simply a matter of a student's personal satisfaction and ambition. As the first president of Rutgers, the Reverend Jacob Hardenbergh, said in a commencement address some 200 years ago, the funds used to provide education for our students "are not properly charity or alms, but money set out at interest [to the benefit of] the whole society." If we do not train these new students to the needs of the technological society we inhabit, we will have lost a vast natural resource of human energy and ability and created a huge reservoir of social alienation arising out of unfulfilled aspiration. Our failure in this respect will be a social tragedy rather than merely an individual loss.

After teaching students, the second great university service to the community is research. I know that some people outside the university are skeptical of the benefits derived from such so-called "pure research," or "ivory tower speculation." Its productive output cannot easily be measured and those who undertake it seem to have what looks to some people like a "very soft berth." This view of the research function of the university is grossly mistaken. In the first place, anyone who wants to remain an effective teacher in higher education, where changes in the system of knowledge are so rapid, must be actively engaged in research. In the second place, I can personally vouch for the fact that the unremitting search after knowledge is as tough and demanding as any work anyone can do anywhere, any time. In the third place, the research done within the university provides much of the intellectual capital on which our society as a whole lives. Just as no modern corporation can compete successfully without applying a significant proportion of its budget to research and development—so-called "R & D"—so too no society can long prosper without encouraging research, the acquisition of new knowledge. Research within the university is the "R & D" arm of the state and society.

During my inaugural in New Brunswick last Wednesday, I pointed out that in recent years too much of the research of the university community—not particularly that of Rutgers, by the way—had been devoted to the uses of war and commercial profit. I believe, as do many others, of course, that it is time for a turn in our national priorities and that this turn should be reflected in changed research priorities funded by the state.

Our megalopolis has questions which cry out for solution. The quality of life in all its dimensions, rather than merely the quantity of goods we produce, should be at the very center of our efforts as a people.

Many research efforts, which are undramatic and deemed unrewarding at the time they are undertaken, may ultimately prove to be spectacularly successful. Look, if you will, at Selman Waksman's discovery of streptomycin, which took place in your state university. It seemed like any other work in the "ivory tower" of the laboratory until it yielded extraordinary results, which remade the world of medicine and won for its discoverer a Nobel Prize.

Relatively small sums of money applied to research in the university can yield fantastically high returns. The state and industry must harness the research capacity of our university to solve the problems of our cities and suburbs. Recall what university research did for agriculture in this state. Then apply the same formula of support to the needs of the megalopolis. The analogy is not a precise one of course. But it is a suggestive one, which should be pursued if this state is to meet the needs of its people and provide for the general welfare.

The last of the three missions of the university is to serve community needs directly by applying knowledge to social uses. I do not mean that the university can or should be a major social service agency. It does not have the resources to undertake such a task. Moreover, it is not especially well-equipped for it, and its capacity to fulfill its other roles would be severely impaired if it undertook social service on a disproportionally large scale.

Having established these limits on the university's direct community service involvement, let me go on to describe the exciting, appropriate and highly significant work which can and should be done in this area.

Again the analogy of university service to the farm community is a helpful one. Besides establishing an agricultural experiment station for research into farm problems, this legislature also established and funded an agricultural extension service whose role it was to bring research results directly to the fields, farmhouses and dairy barns of the state. The result has been a remarkably successful wedding of theory and practice on the farmlands.

We cannot promise exactly the same result from extension work on the problems of the megalopolis.

Many of them are more difficult and the level of development of research on their solution is not as immediately promising. But we should nevertheless pursue such extension work in relation to the problems of the megalopolis. Not to do so would be to serve the cities and suburbs in a lesser way than we served our farms. Not to do so would be to abandon a major source of hope without having anything more promising to replace it.

We have faculty, student and administrators who feel a profound sense of responsibility in respect to the plight of urbanized America and New Jersey. They have knowledge and skills which can and should be brought to bear. Such an application would test and perfect their academic capacities in the cauldron of daily life. It would also enable them to express their outrage over human suffering and injustice in a constructive and significant way. We in the state university should be extending our partnership with state agencies. Our schools of social work and education, our Bureau of Community Services and our urban research and teaching divisions should be fashioning and operating nursery school programs in cooperation with the Department of Education and the Department of Community Affairs. The divisions of the university which study and teach politics should be serving this legislature and local communities as bureaus of legislative reference. Our science and engineering departments should be working with the

Department of Environmental Protection to over-come threats to our environment.

The examples of such co-operative effort could be extended endlessly. The point is simply this: the university has knowledge and skills which the urban and suburban centers of this state could use construc-tively. Such extension work is already being done. The state and university must find ways to enlarge and perfect this effort to cope with the problems of its cities and suburbs.

We cannot promise utopian or apocalyptic results. We can look forward, however, to modest and highly constructive gains. Extending the opportunity for a university education on a fair and equitable basis to all citizens of New Jersey who are qualified to under-take it, transforming our university research priori-ties to meet the special needs of our megalopolis, and providing the benefits of applied research through an urban and suburban extension service—these are the ways the university has been serving and will continue to serve this state.

We recognize, of course, that the enlargement of the mission of the university will require increased financial support by the state. We acknowledge, how-ever, that we can only seek such increased support after we examine all our current programs and in-crease their efficiency and eliminate those which are least productive. We are currently re-examining our tuition policy with an eye to the possibility of placing some larger portion of the cost of higher education on those who can afford to pay it and on those who benefit most directly from their education. However, I strongly urge the legislature and the executive branch not to impose such a tuition increase on us precipitously. Give us time to study the problem carefully. Tuition in a state university is really just another form of taxation. Without adequate study, an across-the-board tuition increase will simply fall most heavily and retrogressively on those least able to pay it. Unless I am mistaken it will fall most heavily on the poor and the white lower middle class, who are already sorely burdened by taxation and already finding it difficult if not impossible to meet educational costs.

Finally, in this regard, it is important to note that many people in the state recognize that neither higher education nor other necessary state services can receive the enlarged support from the state they require until the tax base of the state is drastically restructured. The current extraordinary reliance on local property taxes is recognized widely as inadequate and inequitable. We in the university pin our hopes on the State Tax Policy Committee, the Governor and the new legislature to right this wrong. This state has the third highest per capita income of any state in the nation. It should be able to afford and take pride in a state university and a higher education system commensurate with its stature and its financial capacity. Reform of our tax structure is the very condition for accomplishing this. We trust that men and women of good will in both parties will come forward without political partisanship to undertake this task.

New Jersey is a great state, ranking among the wealthiest, most productive and most populous in the nation. Its people want and require a great state university, matching their aims, their capacity and their educational aspirations. Together you in the executive and legislative branches of government and we in the state university should build a greater university in service to a greater state.

Part II
The Student
Counterculture

The New Student

IN HIS STUDY OF LIFE in the France of Louis XIV, entitled *The Splendid Century* (1957), W. H. Lewis describes with a fine irony the growing revolutionary sentiment of the French peasantry:

> And then there was a nasty spirit abroad in the village; the people were getting impudent, slacker about paying their feudal dues, and sulking about the performance of Manorial Corvées. In some districts peasants have begun "to stare proudly and insolently" at their lord, and are "putting their hands in their pockets instead of saluting him. . . . A noble has been executed for squeezing his peasants a little too hard; it is becoming quite common for peasants to go to law with their seigneur. Things have come to a pretty pass in France."

Based upon an address delivered on May 9, 1968, at the University of Illinois Law School, Urbana, Illinois.

31

And so too have things come to a pretty pass in American higher education! There is a nasty spirit abroad on the college campus; students are growing impudent: sulking and unwilling simply to attend classes and take notes, they are protesting, striking, sitting-in, demanding a voice in the governance of their colleges, staring proudly and insolently at college presidents and professors alike.

American colleges and universities are undergoing a constitutional crisis. Students are seeking a new role in academic life. The purpose of this paper is to inquire into the causes and the nature of student assertion of a right to share in the management of the American college and university.

The classical American college, against which the ire of students is directed, was a place of serene social relationships and scholarly detachment. Trustees, presidents, faculty and students each had a well-established place in a well-ordered hierarchy. Self-appointed trustees, acting as representatives of the general public or some specialized religious community, determined the goals of the college and hired a president to implement these chosen goals. The president then hired a faculty to teach what he believed had to be taught, and he admitted students to the college to learn what he believed had to be learned.

President, faculty and students lived together in the bucolic isolation of their campus, each fulfilling a pre-established role in a universe ordered by the trustees' vision. Students were responsible to the faculty for fulfilling their academic duties and to the president and his staff for living the life of gentlemen. Faculty were responsible to the president for fulfilling their teaching duties and comporting themselves as scholars and men of good breeding. And, finally, the president was responsible to the trustees for maintaining the internal harmony of the system and directing it towards its ordained ends.

The congruity and consistency of this classical academic community was assured as much by its system of educational values as it was by its hierarchical structure. The intention and unifying purpose of the institution was to transmit a received system of learning and culture. The knowledge to be transmitted was considered to be relatively fixed and it was systematically arranged into convenient and appropriate subject-matter areas, one relating to another in the same harmonious order found in nature. The social tradition which was to be inculcated was likewise characterized by its fixity and its conformity to well-established social expectations.

The student's role in this classical college is simple to describe. A college education was available to and important for a relatively small segment of the population; learning the liberal arts was considered a costly luxury. The student was thus doubly privileged: privileged to be among those chosen to attend college at all, and in attendance at college because he was privileged to be among those who could afford to do so. And, of course, the one privilege reinforced the other.

The privileged student did not go to college; he was sent. His relationship to the college was a contractual one, and the contract concerned was what lawyers term a third-party beneficiary contract. Under such a contractual scheme, one party obliges himself to another to have that other party provide a benefit in goods or services to some third party. In this instance, parents paid tuition to the college in consideration of the college's providing a benefit for their child by educating him.

Since they carried somewhat the sense of a charitable relationship, the early history of such third-party beneficiary contracts—the history relevant for our purposes in this paper—left no room to the beneficiary, the object of charity, to have a voice over any incidents of the contract. Appropriate to this tradition of the law of contracts as well as to his status as a privileged person, the student was in no position to require anything of his college or to enforce obligations against it; he simply accepted the education given to him.

Still another factor explains the passivity and docility of the traditional student. He was young in an age in which youth was not in fashion and at a time when parents took an assertive and autocratic stance

towards their children. It is, I know, difficult for us
any longer to evoke the sense of that day when parents were true parents and when being young, although not a disease, was still considered an incapac-
ity. There can be no legitimate doubt, however, that
this facet of the cultural climate underlay and reinforced the traditional student's sense of his servile,
childlike status in his relationship to his college.

It is not difficult to understand how, under these
circumstances, the doctrine of *in loco parentis* grew,
flourished and came to embody the college's conception of its relation to its students. Dealing with young
people in a day when it still rang true to say "children are to be seen, but not heard," educating them
under a third-party beneficiary contract enforceable
only by a parent, and recognizing them as among a
class privileged to be in college at all, it seemed natural, appropriate and just to look on the college as
the student's substitute parent. The parent having
given over his child to the college authorities for the
purpose of his education, these authorities came to
act in lieu of parents, empowered by law, custom and
usage to direct and control student conduct to the
same extent a parent could.

The fitting image is of the college president as the
academic father and students as the dutiful children
of learning: he had to be wise in his choice of what
the young ones were to study; dedicated and enlight-
ened in his mission as moral guardian over them;

stern but just as their disciplinarian; and yet a man sufficiently attached to life's joy, to provide his young with wholesome and healthy—necessarily nonsexual —outlets for fun and games.

This is the picture of the "classical" college president and his academic wards. Students either had to fit into this picture or else they left the sacred academic precincts. They had no other choice than, in the words of the Illinois Supreme Court written in the dark era, to "yield obedience to those who, for the time being, are their master."

There are those, I am certain, who look back longingly to the classical American college, in which trustees, president, faculty and students, each knowing where each belonged, revolved about the central sun of certain knowledge in orbital harmony. My own evocation of the past of our colleges serves an entirely different need, however. For one thing, I have no regret over the old order's having passed; what praise it merits for its stability and fixity of purpose is surely overbalanced by its intellectual anemia, its myopic vision of its social function and its insufferable class bias. For another thing, however, for good or for ill, the winds of change have blown; and we must look to what is past not to savor it or forswear it, but to learn what we can from it.

To be sure, the view which I have presented of what I have called the classical American college is incomplete and wanting; it is a kind of historical caricature. Like other caricatures, however, it is intended to grasp and emphasize what is essential, even if it does so at the expense of some distortion. What marked the classical college was an hierarchical structure of authority, a fixed and ordered system of certain knowledge, a rigidly defined and severely limited set of educational functions, and a completely paternalistic relationship between student and college. The breakdown of the classical college system and the emergence of the new student may be traced, among other causes, to weaknesses in each of these characteristic elements of it.

This is not the place, of course, to discuss all of the causes of the dissolution of the classical system and the emergence of modern colleges and universities. It is enough for my purposes here to examine three of the chief engines of change: expansion in and transformation of the character of the body of knowledge the university is called upon to nurture and transmit, the development of the social function education is called upon to perform, and the emergence of the new student. Each of these changes has profoundly affected the organizational structure of the academic community and the student's role in it.

Contemporary knowledge is more a congeries of discrete and specialized truths than a unified system; and the congeries keeps growing and growing in size and complexity. Moreover, the extent of what we know is such that few men can profess to anything but a relatively narrow segment of the body of our knowledge. Still further, we may say that, with the exception of mathematics and the subject areas it touches, deductive certainty has played a more and more insignificant role as a style of thought; tentative empirical hypotheses, shifting and changing explanations of observable facts, have come to typify our way of thinking. The final characteristic of contemporary knowledge which is significant in this context is that it has become increasingly useful to and important for us. Knowledge is a necessity of life in the intricate social, political and economic structure of the contemporary world.

Each of these characteristics of the corpus of our knowledge has had a marked effect on the college community. No longer can a board of trustees and a college president pretend to even a bare acquaintance with, much less a mastery over, the range of subjects the college teaches. Their attempts to manage and oversee what is taught necessarily reflect this fact. Under the circumstances, the faculty must look to their peers, within and without the college, for guidance and supervision in the performance of their teaching functions. And this, of course, represents a radical breach in the classical scheme of the organization of the college. Faculties can no longer be responsible, in any realistic sense, to presidents and lay boards for what they teach and how they teach it.

Still another consequence of the changed character

of contemporary knowledge is that the curriculum has lost both its unity and what I might call its pre-emptive character. The complexity, diversity and specialization of contemporary thought make it impossible to fix upon any single set or even any small number of sets of subjects of study which can be considered basic or fundamental to higher education. Under these circumstances, method and the process of inquiry are bound to take on more importance than subject-matter competence. And the varied interests, skills, capacities and inclinations of students come to be a more significant determinant of what they should study than any predetermined fixed order of universally prescribed courses.

The impact of this on the organization of the college is once again to impair the classical hierarchy of dominance and control. Those who would prescribe a course of study, whether boards, presidents or faculty, are increasingly at a loss to say what is to be prescribed. The very diversity and specialization of what we teach in the contemporary college makes it impossible to lay down with any assurance what anyone should learn.

This same influence on attempts to prescribe a settled curriculum arises from the empirical and non-deductive character of our knowledge. Instead of a single corpus of learning strictly ordered by the canons of logic and carrying the weight of an established tradition, we find discrete and shifting sets or families of theories, only loosely bound together and constantly shifting, as observation and new theoretical insight restructure entire fields of science. Who shall say, who can say, what is settled and enduring, what is fundamental to the educational process, in the face of this? Whoever has insight into this facet of the logic, the history and the sociology of knowledge must in modesty confess that attempts at prescribing a fixed and universal curricular organon are doomed to failure.

I suggest then, that the constitutional structure of the classical college has been impaired in two important respects by the development of our system of knowledge. The claim on the part of lay boards and presidents to exercise exclusive control over what is taught and how it is taught in the college has given way simply on account of obvious, though, of course, far from blameworthy, incompetence. And the boards' and presidents'—even the faculty's—claim to exercise exclusive control over what must be learned has given way because of the specialization, diversity and shifting empirical character of what is taught.

Although I shall develop this thought as I proceed, I might say in a preliminary fashion, at this point, that the constitutional role of students has been affected by each of these two revisions in the structure of the college community. Once the college faculty has successfully challenged the legitimacy of the board's and the president's exclusive role in determining educational policy, the whole classical structure of authority is threatened and students can begin to ask why boards and presidents should solely determine anything else. This same skeptical and corrosive doubt flows from the increasing weakness evidenced in authoritative attempts to prescribe a curriculum.

The final facet of the development of our system of knowledge which has affected the student's role in his college is directly related to the second major influence mentioned previously as having undermined the classical college. What we teach in colleges has come to have greater and greater utility for our society and this, in turn, has caused our society to look on the college in an entirely new light. Whereas formerly the function the college performed was limited, and of interest to a relatively small segment of the community, the contemporary college and university fulfills a multitude of social tasks which are of considerable importance to the society as a whole.

The traditional college prepared a privileged minority to take roles in society as members of a governing elite and as practitioners of a small number of the genteel professions; the research and scholarship which was done in it bore the mark of its origin in the ivory towers of academia. The burgeoning of knowledge in the physical and social sciences and its usefulness to society at large has now led to the appearance of a whole range of new professions and occupations which engage the interest and capacity of the broadest segments of our population. Moreover, academic research and scholarship now directly service our economy and our political and social life on a vast and unprecedented scale. Educational institutions have become a major and vital national resource rather than a peripheral upper-class luxury.

The transition in the importance of higher education in our national life is shown most graphically by comparison of enrollment figures and by examination of some financial data. The enrollment in colleges and universities in 1869 was 52,000, 0.1 per cent of our general population and 1.1 per cent of the 18–24-year-olds; by 1910, it had grown to 355,000, 0.4 per cent of our general population and 2.9 per cent of the 18–24-year-olds; by 1963, it had grown to 4,234,000, 2.2 per cent of the general population and 23.3 per cent of our 18–24-year-olds.

In terms of public funding of education, the figures are no less dramatic. Until this decade, federal funds expended for higher education were almost negligible. But in 1965, the federal government spent $1.9 billion and in 1966 it spent $2.6 billion directly on higher education. In addition to these funds, the federal government made grants of $3.2 billion in 1965 and $3.6 billion in 1966 to educational institutions for research activities. In these same years, 1965 and 1966, state governments expended $3.9 billion and $4.4 billion respectively for higher education.

Combined state and federal expenditures in these two years represented some fifty-eight per cent of the total cost of higher education in America.

It is plain that, for good or for ill, education has gone public. It is vested with a national interest and increasingly funded out of the public purse. There is every indication that the trend in this direction will increase rather than diminish in the coming years. The consequence of this development is to erode still further the structure of trustee and presidential authority.

Some of the erosion is quite direct, some of it indirect. Most federal funding is advanced for specified educational purposes rather than general operating costs. In the case of research funds, the money most often goes directly to the academic researcher, and the college or university has virtually no control over its expenditure. In the case of other funds, the college can only say yea or nay to a grant for a specific purpose; frequently, considering the penury of most academic budgets, there is really no choice. Thus, trustees and presidents have in good measure been forced to abdicate real control over the expenditure of their own funds to become bookkeepers of public funds.

The indirect effects of the widespread public interest in and support of higher education are even more important for our purposes. Even if federal funding did not limit the trustees' and presidents' available managerial options, it would still vastly diminish their power. Use of public funds in higher education calls for a degree and kind of public accountability, of responsibility to the public at large, which goes far beyond the vague and self-enforced sense which the traditional trustee and president had of representing the community interest. This change is reinforced by the fact that faculty and students alike— the low men on the traditional totem pole of academic power—are part of that public to which the trustee is accountable. Thus, the nature and extent of the trustees' and presidents' authority must necessarily be changed and diminished when they begin to expend and control funds which they do not themselves donate or generate.

Another aspect of the new public interest in education is that it gives college faculty a new sense of their social status, a sense which is at variance with their traditional subservient role in the collegiate hierarchy. They are no longer creatures of a benign alma mater's largesse. They are valued social operatives, sought after to fulfill important tasks in the economy and government and equally sought after by other academic institutions suffering from a faculty shortage caused by swollen enrollments.

No longer will a student look with awe and wonder at the college president and believe that the president controls the destinies of the great scholars with whom students study. Prestigious faculty now make and break colleges, buy and sell college presidents, as they say. Both faculty and students are well aware of this dramatic reversal of position and what its consequences are for the college power structure.

Still another facet of what we might call the nationalization of education is that members of the public in unprecedented numbers and coming from social strata and classes never before heard from in the halls of academia are now personally concerned with collegiate and academic affairs. Government officialdom, employers, professionals, workers, and parents of widely varying backgrounds all now feel a vital interest in a new-found national resource, and they expect it to meet their needs. No longer is the college the preserve of the few, to be watched over and nurtured by magnanimous and wealthy donors and wistful, teary-eyed alumni. The college is everyman's garden to be cared for and intended to suit everyman's taste and interest.

The last of the challenges to the classical college tradition is directed at the conception of the college serving *in loco parentis*—the paternalism embodied in the collegiate hierarchy of authority. This challenge arises from a number of causes: in the first place, the very conception of the rule and authority of parents has changed slowly over a period of time. Increasingly, parents have come to rely on reason and suggestion rather than status and command as the essential elements of control over their children.

Many parents, practicing the cult of permissiveness, have come to eschew any and all forms of discipline; even more have come to use discipline sparingly and only as a last resort. Finding one's self, self-expression and individual development have come to displace parental guidance and social standards of conformity as the molders of character and personality. All of these changes have contributed to the development of a generation of new students who instinctively react against authority, academic or otherwise.

The second cause of the breakdown of the paternalistic pattern of collegiate life is a changed attitude towards the nature of the learning process. The traditional student was a relatively more passive participant in the learning process than is the new student. Memory and deductive forms of reasoning were formerly more important student tools than imagination, observation and criticism. The new student is asked to learn by coping with his subject of study in the same way his teacher does; he is not asked so much to listen to his teacher as to do what his teacher does. He learns by doing and experiencing rather than remembering and deducing. Learning increasingly becomes a form of apprenticeship rather than a form of tutelage.

This changed conception of the learning process finds its way into the earliest school years and reaches its culmination, or should, in college study. Its impact on the constitutional organization of colleges is profound and in many respects similar to that, described above, of the changed character of knowledge systems. Just as the increasing complexity and specialization and the decreasing deductive unity and fixity of knowledge has weakened the authority of those who would pretend to prescribe curricula and otherwise control what is taught, so too the same result arises out of the changed conception of the learning process.

To the degree the student becomes an active and creative element in his own education, rather than a passive recipient in the process, he comes to resist and resent those who seek to determine for him what he should learn. The very intellectual independence and critical judgment which are fostered and desired as tools of learning are corrosive of the authority of faculty and academic administration. "It is so because the president and trustees say so" is no more an answer to be respected in fixing on a course of study or style of life on campus, than "it is so because Aristotle said so" is an answer to be respected in discussion of a philosophical or aesthetic problem in the classroom.

A third factor which tends to undermine the capacity of the college to act as a substitute parent is the new social attitude towards attending college. The traditional student was sent to college by his parents and felt it a privilege to be there. The new student goes to college because he knows it is necessary for him; his parents and, increasingly, his society, pays his way because, under the conditions of modern life, a college education is as much his right as a high school education is.

In these circumstances, the college must begin to regard its role as that of a social agent performing a socially valued function rather than merely that of a private agent of a parent undertaking an educational task the parent pays for. It is not the parent who puts the student into college but society, and in educating a student the college is not acting in the parent's name but in society's.

Moreover, although the student obviously benefits from his education, it is regarded as a necessity rather than a privilege by his society, which also derives benefit from it. The new student's attitude, even when a parent pays for his education, reflects the changed status of education as a social necessity rather than a private luxury in modern life. However thankful and appreciative of his education he may be, the student need not feel that anyone is doing him a remarkable favor for which he must be beholden and for which he must pay by adopting a respectful and deferential attitude towards authority.

Gone then is the older notion of a third-party beneficiary contract in favor of the privileged student who retained no right to control its incidence. In its place is a new status relationship in which the college performs a socially prescribed task in a manner over which the society generally, including the student, retains considerable control. The private contract is now replaced by a public duty. In the transition, the paternalism of the older form of the relationship between student and college has become an anachronism.

The fourth and final cause of the breakdown of collegiate paternalism which I shall examine is the changed character of the student body itself. In the last century, we have experienced almost a hundred-fold increase in the size of our collegiate student body; a change, as I have already indicated, from a student body comprised of 1 per cent of the 18–24-year-olds 100 years ago, to 23.3 per cent of them today. These new students come from social classes and national and racial backgrounds never before present on college campuses in such numbers. They are bright and mature, alienated from traditional values, and newly aware of their political power. This adds up to a radical change in the character of the collegiate student body, and the purport of this change is to strain still further the traditional organization of collegiate authority.

The new student is not older than the traditional student, but he has had more experience of life. He comes from homes and family backgrounds which have been less isolated from the economic and social struggle. The very style of family life in which he has been brought up is more open and honest, has made him more aware of what life is really about. He is a product of a better primary and secondary education. And finally he shows the effect of the communications revolution, for he is a child of television and the film industry.

The sum of these influences has brought forth a generation of young people which is more sensitive to life in all its dimensions than any generation before it has been. These young people have vicariously experienced the whole range of human emotions and been witness to the whole play of political passions. Love and hatred; war, greed and bloodshed; discrimination, hunger and deprivation; electioneering and voting: they have seen it all in ways which were not possible before the advent of the television tube. These new students have gotten the message from the media, and they exhibit its mark by their bearing and purpose.

The second characteristic of the new student which is important for our purposes is his alienation from traditional values and institutions. To be sure, there have been disaffected students before this time. The difference now is in the extent of the disillusion: it is more widespread and it bites more deeply into the range of life's values than it ever has before.

War, poverty, and racial discrimination all loom as fundamental and insurmountable political outrages. Infidelity, divorce, illegitimacy, bureaucratization, and mass conformity appear as poisonous and ineradicable social diseases. And the individual is thought to be inevitably threatened by increasing isolation, loneliness, and boredom. There is nothing to look forward to except losing one's soul in exchange for the dross of material wealth. The old values have failed and there are no new ones to take their place. All the ideologies, all the utopias—from democratic capitalism to Christian salvation to Marxist socialism —seem to have failed. The only heroes left are those who preach destruction, with no other vision of the social good. This is indeed a generation of rebels without a cause, a generation of nihilists, a generation despairing of the life we live and set on remaking it, but without a vision of any alternative.

And yet the new student is a very political person. Again, of course, we can acknowledge the fact that student generations before this have played the political game. The difference here, as with this generation's alienation, is a difference of degree. Not small political cells, nor ineffectual weekly political discussion groups, but impressively large numbers of activists are dedicated with all their being to the pursuit of their political purposes.

In the struggle over the civil rights issue and over the Vietnam war they found a first taste of political success. No other generation of young people in this country has had such political effect, none has been so heralded by journalists or so courted by politicians. They have quite suddenly achieved a sense of their own authority, a sense of the growing force of their own numbers, a sense of identification with the older European and Latin American tradition of student political power. Most important of all, they have developed a distinctive style of political action and a distinctive form of political tactics.

Thus, although the new student is alienated and lacks the conviction of an ideology, he is outraged by evil and thereby transformed into a political person. Disillusioned with traditional political programmatic goals, he stands and fights on limited particular issues. Disillusioned with traditional party and parliamentary politics, he confronts social wrongs directly, attempting limited and immediate remedies. Disillusioned with adult politicians, he has himself become a politician.

The impact of the three characteristics of the new student which I have described on the structure of collegiate authority has been extraordinary. No generation so bright and mature, so alienated from traditional values, and so political in its bearing could conceivably tolerate the paternalism of the classical collegiate system. The new student's maturity and his politicalization, combined with the influence of the other developments which I previously described, make attempts on the part of trustees and administration to prescribe authoritatively courses of study seem ever more illegitimate. The more mature student, seeking to have his education serve his new values and new political goals, wants and needs more of a voice in what he shall study and what the educational goals and values of the college shall be.

As for parietal rules, these seem ever more absurd. The values and style of life embodied in the campus rules of the "Old Coll" were born of a different time, a time which had not yet seen the unmasking of the sexual hypocrisy of the adult world, a time in which college students were tender and innocent young things who had to be protected from evil. The new student, coming frequently from a different class and culture than the traditional student, is deeply impressed by the contrast in his values and those embodied in the rules of tne traditional college. He is suspicious of the trustees and the college president because they are representatives of a value system and of a time he is in the act of rejecting. Under the circumstances, he sees no good reason to accept the authority of the trustees and college president over the conditions of his social life.

The intransigence of the classical collegiate system in the face of these student claims for new freedom and power has reinforced the strains of the underlying conflict. An unheeding structure of collegiate authority has caused the new student to begin to look upon college life as a replica of the wider world from which he is alienated. Trustees and presidents begin to assume the aspect of authoritarian oppressors, enforcing their own system of values on oppressed and powerless students, robbing them of their dignity and impairing their opportunity to pursue the true academic life. Faculty begin to appear to have sold out and abandoned their calling; instead of serving as prophets of a new and better world, they have been seduced into collaboration with the military-industrial establishment by the lure of lucrative contracts. The curriculum comes to seem empty and unimportant, out of tune with our times, irrelevant to our agonies and needs. The goals and purposes of colleges and universities seem to have been subverted from open-minded criticism of the established social order to authoritarian forms of protection and service of that conservative order. And underneath all these other appearances, there is the specter of the university as a bureaucratic machine controlled by irresponsible elites and as petty, inhuman, undemocratic and unresponsive as the world beyond the ivy-covered walls.

A structure of constitutional authority is a delicate thing. Compounded of force and implicit threats of force, of unquestioning acquiescence, habitual obedience, unresponsiveness to felt need, and an aura of moral fitness, it can only persist if each of these elements continues to contribute its saving balance. It now seems plain that the traditional hierarchical organization of collegiate power must either deliberately readjust to new realities or be transmuted by the impact of discontent.

Radical changes in the system of knowledge, in the social interest in knowledge, and in the student population have all combined to unhinge the delicate balance of academic authority. Acquiescence in, and habitual obedience to, the traditional structure have begun to dissolve under the actuality of a new relationship of faculty and students to presidents and trustees. The unresponsiveness of academic authority to the needs of students and to the changed conditions of academic life has slowly eroded the sense of that authority's moral fitness to govern. Under the circumstances, no matter how strong the force used or threatened, the college and university can never be the same again.

Student activists as well as apologists and defenders of the traditional order are both mistaken about the character of the constitutional revolution in academia. The activists, whether out of ignorance or assumed tactical necessity, conjure up images of the college more appropriate to a hundred years ago than today, and they urge political tactics as mistaken as their image of the college.

As with all revolutions, the seeds of this one were laid over a long period of time, and the foundations of the old order have long since been undermined by the growth of new sprouts of faculty and student authority. Trustees and presidents of a number of institutions have long since abandoned in fact, if not in law, any pretensions to absolute power and have been seeking diligently for a new form of order. Thus, what Riesman and Jencks call "the academic revolution" is proceeding apace. The need now is as much to consolidate and give structure to changes which have already taken place as it is to exert the pressure of opinion against enclaves of the old tradition. Deliberation about and thoughtful discussion of the new constitutional order should have as high a priority as strident demands and militant tactics against the old constitutional order.

Once it is agreed, as many would now agree, that trustees and presidents can no longer exercise absolute power over the acamedic world, once it is agreed that faculty and students must play a real and substantial role in academic government, a whole series of profound and complex problems arise. How precisely shall power be distributed among trustees, presidents, faculty and students? If the hierarchical structure of power is inappropriate, what should replace it? What is the appropriate sphere of each of the organs of power and how are the relationships between these organs and their various jurisdictions to be arranged?

Many colleges and universities are already deeply involved in addressing themselves to these issues and others like them. Some are doing this quite consciously; others as a facet of unconscious throes of change and transition, while still maintaining the fiction of the traditional structure.

Many a revolution has been lost after it had succeeded because those who favored and fought for change neglected to concern themselves with what was to follow the disappearance of the old order. It would be folly of the gravest character to undo the traditional academic structure only to have it replaced with one less just and more inadequate.

One of the most significant dangers we face in this regard is that some of the very tactics used to complete the work of reordering the structure of academic authority promise to prejudice the result unalterably. To be sure, there is still resistance in the academic world to abandoning the old forms of authority. And to be sure, this resistance must be overcome by organized political effort. But if there was ever a political struggle in which violence and illegality were unnecessary and inappropriate, this is one. If there was ever a political struggle in which violence and illegality were calculated to destroy the very fruits of victory which are sought, this is one.

The fact is that, for the reasons I have set forth at length, the traditional forms of power are already fast crumbling. The change is already in the works and its pace is quickening. Allies in the form of sympathetic trustees, presidents, and faculty are at hand. Tactics of violence are antithetical to deliberation, the very essence of the academic life. Under the circumstances, students with romantic, stereotyped, and anachronistic conceptions of revolution, students whose need to undertake violent political action is more a function of personal and emotional, rather than political, necessity should exercise restraint over their revolutionary fantasies. The violence they unleash may, on occasion, produce a temporary aura of success, but it threatens the long-range prospects for building the college and university we desire. As Paul Goodman put it in a slightly different context: "Out of the shambles can only come the same bad world."

Defenders of the old order also suffer under a number of illusions. The first and most important of these is that the whole "fuss," "the so-called revolt," is the work of a few ill-mannered, loud-mouthed radicals. The truth of the matter is, however, that revolutions call forth leaders; leaders never call forth revolution. Leaders can never create social upheaval; they can ride its crest.

As I have shown in the main body of this paper, the erosion of the traditional structure of academic authority which we are presently witnessing flows from developments in the character of knowledge, in the social uses to which knowledge is put, and in the psychology of our students. It is these underlying social facts which are responsible for transforming the academic world rather than any group of student leaders. Even if all our student activists were to disappear miraculously, the fundamental maladjust-

ment in the organization of collegiate power would
remain.

Too many of our academic leaders have mistaken
the true nature of the student revolt. They are confused because at different times it appears to be ad-
dressed to one or another of different, relatively insignificant or, even when not insignificant, relatively
isolated, facets of college life. First it is free speech
on campus, then it is visitation hours in student
rooms, then admissions and scholarships for black
students, then recruitment of students by war indus-
tries, then the building of a gymnasium in an urban
slum, then the contract relationship between the
university and a defense research corporation. The
connection between these seemingly isolated forays
is that they all represent a testing of the academic
decision process; they all go to challenge the legitimacy of the constitutional apparatus of the college
or university.

These incidents are not only related to each other,
but they are also related to the more profound challenges posed to the structure of the college which
I have discussed above. In other words, the student
activists have chosen to throw the gauntlet down, not
only on issues which have extraordinary immediate
political appeal, but also on issues which go to test
the academic hierarchy and thereby reinforce and
find reinforcement from the underlying causes of im-

balance in the structure of academic authority. A failure to appreciate these relationships promises a failure to be able to cope successfully with the problems they present.

A related facet of the misunderstanding of the nature of the student revolt concerns an underestimation of the amount of support it finds on university campuses and elsewhere. It is significant and symbolic of this failure generally that the police, who had been called to cope with disturbances on the Columbia University campus and did a poor job of it, complained that their failure was attributable in part to the fact that the administration of the college had grossly underestimated the number of students who were "sitting-in" in their buildings.

I am certain that the experience at Columbia will turn out, after we have studied it, to be much like that at Berkeley in that—as the Muscatine Report demonstrates—the activists "succeeded" because they had wide support, not only among students generally, but among faculty and among the lay public as well. The reason for this support at Berkeley, Columbia, and elsewhere is not only traceable to the appeal of the particular political issues on which the ruckuses were raised, but also to the fact that the issues concerned evoked the support of all those—faculty, students, and laymen alike—who questioned the underlying structure of collegiate authority.

The second important illusion under which many

defenders of the traditional college suffer concerns remedies. There are some "academic statesmen"— fortunately few in number—who insist that, if the students do not appreciate what they have, let them leave or be "kicked out" and that this will represent a solution to the contemporary crisis. After all, they add, students do not attend college under coercion; if they do not choose to conform let them leave.

I believe that some students should indeed be disciplined and more generally that the order of the college community should be maintained during this difficult transition period. There are indeed a number of students who, because of political naïveté, political romanticism, or plain malevolence, are bent on destroying what most needs to be saved and rebuilt. And there are a greater number of other students who find in the contemporary situation of stress a rationalization for ill-mannered, selfish, and boorish disregard of the rights of others. But anyone who supposes that by disciplining such students we will have solved the crisis of academic authority is grossly mistaken. Its roots, as I have shown, go much deeper.

Nor do I believe—and I note my judgment is somewhat tentative on this score—we are very much nearer a solution by providing students "means to participate in the formulation and application of institutional policy affecting academic and student affairs," providing forms of due process in disciplinary proceedings, and removing all restraints on students' freedom to express themselves. These were the major recommendations of the "Joint Statement on Rights and Freedoms of Students," [1] issued by the Association of American Colleges, the United States National Student Association, the American Association of University Professors and a number of other academic groups. As admirable and helpful as this statement is, and as strongly as I applaud the good judgment and diligence of those who produced it, I must conclude it is of peripheral interest in the context of the constitutional challenge American colleges and universities presently face.

The weakness of the "Joint Statement" resides in the vagueness of the language used to define the character of the student role and in the fact that even this obscure statement was further emasculated in the resolution of endorsement by the Association of American Colleges. A "means to participate in the formulation and application of institutional policy" —the language of the "Joint Statement"—is not the same as the assurance of some form of shared control or authority over institutional policy. In fact, it might be interpreted by some as more of the "let's pretend" theory of student government, more a form of "manipulated acquiescence," than a true grant of a significant share of power.

This appearance of weakness is underscored further by the fact that the resolution of endorsement

[1] *Liberal Education,* LIV (March, 1968), pp. 152–158.

of the Association of American Colleges limits the language of the "Joint Statement" by providing that the student participation concerned—and I quote the "Resolution of Endorsement"—"may involve a variety of activities, under methods appropriate to each campus, ranging from student discussion of proposed policy in committees, in organized agencies of student government or through the student press to the more formal determination of policy by groups that include student members or, where and if delegated by appropriate authority, by groups that are composed only of students" (pp. 144–146). Thus, it turns out that the colleges which endorsed the "Joint Statement" made little or no definitive commitment to the doctrine of shared power. In all probability the "Joint Statement" represents only a commitment to freedom of expression and opportunities for joint discussion; at most, it is a commitment, under some circumstances, to the joint or sole exercise by students of delegated power.

What the "Joint Statement" seems oblivious of is that the crucial issue before American colleges and universities is not due process, freedom of expression, or even forms of delegated representation, as important as these are. What is rather at issue is who shall retain ultimate control and sovereignty over the academic institution; what is at issue is whose goals, values, and objectives the college and university shall serve.

Due process in disciplinary proceedings and freedom of expression can help to assure that organs of power are responsive to the interests of those they serve. Representation on decision-making bodies whose authority is delegated by the ultimate organs of power can serve the same function even more effectively. But both of these political means fall short of reconstituting the organs of power themselves, fall short of changing the nature of ultimate sovereignty. As long as the power to be exercised by students—or faculty, for that matter—is solely delegated power rather than a share of ultimate power, the basic nature of their relationship to sovereign power remains untouched.

Thus, although the "Joint Statement" takes a significant step towards creating a more responsive academic government, it does not touch the problem of creating a more truly responsible academic government. In the long run, no institution can remain sufficiently responsive to those it serves, however well-intentioned and however well managed, unless it is responsible to them. And it can only be responsible to them if they share, in one way or another, in the ultimate disposition and control of power.

A share of delegated authority may assure responsiveness, but it is not to be confused with a share of the power to delegate authority, which is the reservoir of ultimate power. Only a share in that ultimate power can truly assure responsible government, rather than merely responsive government.

In conclusion, I would urge that student activists and protectors of the old order alike have mistaken the true nature of the student revolt: the student activists, because they do not sufficiently realize that the movement to reorganize the collegiate constitution had begun long before they came on the scene, that it has already progressed far beyond their wildest dreams, and that some of their tactics are inimical to its success. For their part, the protectors of the old order are mistaken about the true character of the revolt, its extent, and the kinds of remedies which are appropriate. Let us all get over our illusions and begin the difficult work of redefining the nature and character of ultimate authority in the academic world.

Distrust between Parents and Their Children

WHY DO ADULTS feel beleaguered by the youth of today in ways they never have before? After all, generational strife is not a novel phenomenon. We can each remember our own youthful struggles against our parents and "their world." Many of us lived through a period of disillusion and disenchantment with the adult establishment. We went on to learn its rules and ways, however, and to succeed at those rules and ways. We then attempted to change some of them in order that the world we passed on to our children would be a better place than the one we inherited.

Our children seem to be taking a different tack. A very few of them want to destroy violently our adult culture. Many of them do not even want to

Look Magazine article, January 26, 1971.

learn our rules and ways. They seem to want to opt out of the struggle of accommodation to the adult world and to find an entirely new life-style. They do not want to succeed; not even to succeed in order to change the system. They want no part of our world; they simply want a way out of its compulsions. Why are they so different from what we were?

Our youth find themselves in a world dominated as never before by bureaucracy and technology. It is a world in which science and rationality have become gods for men to worship rather than tools for men to use. It is a world in which creature comforts and material goods have been sought, produced and accumulated out of all proportion to their appropriate place in the life of man. Finally, it is a world in which the adult population has suffered a failure of nerve, a failure of confidence in its capacity to succeed according to its own lights. These four interrelated factors explain why so many of our youth either withdraw into anomie or express an angry urge to undertake a totally new life-style rather than merely another generational modification of the old one.

The psychiatrist Bruno Bettelheim has characterized the response of young people to modern technology as one of becoming aware of their own obsolescence. The young have a vision of society dominated by the machinery of mass production and computerization, in which individuals and individuality no longer count. It is a society dominated exclusively by mechanical reason, in which emotion no longer counts. They feel like meaningless interchangeable digits in such a world; obsolete as individuals, because in a machine and in a computer, reason obviates human emotion and one individual doesn't mean anything different from another.

This technological society educates young people for what seems like an endless time in order to have them become faceless adults serving the machine. There is no place to go, and they must wait indefinitely to get there. An enforced and overly prolonged adolescence becomes increasingly degrading because it is a period of dependence and deferred gratification. Young people always seem to be preparing for something, waiting, but never quite becoming anything, and fearing that what they might become—images of their parents—isn't worth becoming.

As they wait to enter a world they did not make and do not relish, the young rebels are urged at every turn to succumb to its blandishments. The consumer society pushes its products on them, asking them to consume, consume, consume, never giving them a chance to produce, to do honest human work with a shovel or a pot and pan. They are deprived of the luxury of wanting and hungering after things, and they have an unmistakable urge to vomit out the consumables that they have been force-fed.

This explains what is so ironic to some and so incomprehensible to others: that the most extreme young rebels are almost exclusively children of the middle and upper classes. The rebels are middle- and upper-class kids because it is middle- and upper-class parents who in their lives and the way they have reared their children display the worst features of a society corrupted by materialism.

The contemporary adult world has undergone an overwhelming loss of confidence in itself. In André Malraux's words, "Western civilization has begun to doubt its own credentials." Beset by gnawing anxiety, the guilt-ridden parent overacts and overcompensates; he feeds his child too much and buys him too many gifts; he fears his child and, in response to his own fear, he either becomes a demonic taskmaster to his child or a piece of putty to be reshaped to his child's every desire. He drinks like a fish while preaching the sins of marijuana. He is loose, lewd and lascivious because he is truly afraid of sexual pleasure; yet he preaches purity and abstinence. He hates work, but in order to succeed, continually overworks, and he looks forward to his son's replacing him. His life is filled with the material rewards of his daily rat race, to the exclusion of all other human values, and yet he speaks of himself as a religious man and a true believer in spiritual values.

Can such a father bring up anything but a rebel?

Of course, the portrait I have drawn is a caricature, but like all social caricatures, it projects truth as others see and respond to it. This is the caricature that many of our young carry in their heads. If there are enough points of resemblance to make you squirm, you can understand why our middle- and upper-class children have become potent carriers of what the historian, Theodore Roszak, calls a "counter culture," or what the writer, Paul Goodman, calls "the new reformation."

We parents have literally generated our own rebels. Although in many instances our children do not condemn us as individuals, but love us, our world and its values no longer command their respect. Essentially, they are in rebellion against us and everything for which we stand. This is why the Woodstock rock music festival and others like it can teach us so much about our children. As a symbol of a generation, it is as exaggerated as the portrait I have just drawn of a parent. But all the elements of the counterculture, of what some call the Woodstock Nation, were there to be seen.

The emotional frenzy defied the overbearing and self-righteous equanimity of rationalists and technologists. The open and honest use of drugs and the earthy indulgence in sexual play flew in the face of adult hypocrisy. The overpowering loud and aesthetically innocent music blotted out thought and literally impelled movement and feeling. The childlike nakedness, the bizarre clothing and the outrageous hair worn as badges of identification, as the uniform of this new rebel army, rivaled the uniform of the clean-cut technician in gray flannel suit or white laboratory coat.

The extraordinary abandon of it all, the absence of standards, was a reaction to an adult world that is so standard- and status-conscious it graduates its children from kindergarten and gives doctorates in poultry science. The sense of ambience, of being warm and accepted as somebody by everybody, was a striking contrast to the sterile impersonality and callous rejection people suffer in the machine world of the technologist. Who cared about material comforts, about being somebody, or preparing for something, or arranging or moderating anything at Woodstock?

The Woodstock Nation is not a place for me; nor do I think it an appropriate place for my children. If this be the counterculture, I reject it. There is some charm and delight to it; even significant and attractive values in it. But on the whole, the Woodstock Nation is as depraved and as absurd as the Nation we adults already inhabit.

Imagine, if you will, a rediscovery of individuality that is compulsion-ridden in its attachment to a bizarre style of dress; imagine a profession of humanism that relegates reason, surely one of man's proudest attributes, into the nether world. Imagine seeking joy in sexuality surrounded by hordes of people, or seeking privacy in crowds. Imagine celebrating human consciousness and then drugging yourself into a stupor. Imagine a world so insecure in its own values that it will accept no standards, not even sane and human ones; a world so insecure in its own professions of faith in individuals that it will not admit of some being better, wiser, more gifted or learned than others. Imagine a world that will rock to music, but only if it is loud and simple: that will be moved by ideas, but only if they appear as captions in a cartoon, or as commercials on television. Imagine a world that denigrates words, books and history.

To an extraordinary degree, the Woodstock Nation is a mirror image of the very adult world it rejects. It substitutes one set of distortions of the human spirit for another. Nevertheless, I believe it would be a grave mistake for the adult world, or for any particular parent, to reject the Woodstock Nation or its children out of hand. On the contrary, we desperately need each other in order to make sense of our modern world.

The reason we adults must rediscover our young is twofold. First, they can provide us with moral vision and perspective. They have learned that we emperors of the world have no clothes on; they have seen vividly and surely that the structure of contemporary society is corrupted and debased, a fact that would have been obvious to us long ago if we, like them, had been born into our world, instead of having grown up with it and in it.

Second, having achieved this critical insight, and having been moved to anger, contempt and fury by it, makes our young into a potent political force, a revolutionary one, if you will. They can provide us with the political and social leverage that will re-make our world in the latter part of this century.

But if they are really to succeed, they need our help. We must wed our experience to their energy, our learning to their imagination, our technique to their impulse, our political convictions to their moral intuitions. We have the historical perspective, the knowledge and the political skills that our children lack. If once they recognize we truly share the same ideals and are enlisted in the same cause, they will respond to us as parents and adults, inviting the assistance and support they need and yearn for.

Herman Melville once described a desperate youth going to sea, and he then went on to say that going to sea was the youth's "substitute for pistol and ball." The youth of our nation are desperate, but unlike the youth of Melville's time, they cannot put to sea. We must provide a moral and emotional equivalent to violence, a moral and emotional equivalent to the "pistol and ball." That equivalent is a new politics, a youth strategy, instead of a Southern strategy. We must lead our youth or they will be misled. We must give democratic political form to their inchoate rage.

It will not be easy to create the new political coali-tion and to bridge the gap that has grown between the young and old. We must start at the level of the family and work up through every other social structure in which adults and youth face each other across the chasm of distrust. At each of these levels, the remedy is the same. We parents and adults will have to abandon our hypocrisy and be brutally honest with ourselves and our children about our failures, personal, social and political; and our children will have to abandon their sanctimonious tone and their romantic yearning for a political and social apocalypse. We parents and adults will have to abandon the notion that the claims of success, reason and order are universal, exhaustive and inexorable. And our children will have to abandon their passion for instant gratification and their flirtation with mysticism as a way of life.

These are difficult things to do. But there is no other path to the re-establishment of mutual respect between parents and their children, adults and young people. We must simply work at it together, using as our fundamental tools love and honesty. The alternative is the continuing disintegration of our families, our political institutions and our society.

Who Are the Students and What Do They Want?

WHO ARE THE STUDENTS of the contemporary university and what do they seek in the university? Ten years ago these questions would have seemed out of place. The students of most colleges and universities were a fairly homogeneous lot of white middle- and upper-class youngsters, and they enrolled with one of two overriding purposes, to be liberally educated for a leadership role in a stable society, a business, or to prepare for one of a limited number of professional careers.

All of this has now changed. The students of American universities come to us from every class and condition of society and increasingly from among every race and creed of man. Instead of educating

Inaugural Convocation Address delivered on November 11, 1971, in Symphony Hall, Newark, New Jersey.

some five per cent or less of 18-to-24-year-olds, we now provide higher education for some thirty per cent of that age group. Their educational aspirations and goals have also significantly changed. New personal, vocational and professional aspirations have emerged, and liberal education has increasingly become the condition for upward social mobility and social change rather than a mere gloss for those whose position was already established in a fixed social order. They take the university seriously because in truth their futures depend on it.

This transformation in the character of the student body of American universities has been taking place over a considerable period of time. Unfortunately, however, we have only recently begun to look at it closely and only recently have we begun to be aware of its implications for higher education. In my view, our failure to take this change fully enough into account at an early enough time explains in some large measure the turmoil and sense of unease which has existed on most campuses for some time. We have been trying to put new wine into old bottles, new students into old educational forms, and it simply cannot be done. Our old educational forms must adjust to our new students and their new needs.

Higher education must simply face the fact that its current student body is no longer homogeneous. We must give up talking about "the student" as if there were an eternal Platonic form which epitomized all students. Moreover, we must also recognize that more than ever before our students are extremely volatile, subject to instant change. The future happens more quickly these days; student attitudes come and go at an extraordinary pace, and only awareness of the phenomenon of rapid change will enable us to accommodate to it without future shock.

Who, then, are our students? There are four different groups of students who presently inhabit the campuses of America. There are poor and lower-middle-class whites, poor and lower-middle- and middle-class blacks and Puerto Ricans, alienated children of the white middle and upper classes and nonalienated children of these same white middle and upper classes. Each of these groups is important to us; each must be served by us.

Before attempting to characterize further these groups of students, I want to state what will already be obvious to most of you. These categories are not airtight nor do they comprehend the entire range of students. Some students, in other words, will not fit in any one of them while some students will display characteristics of more than one of them. Of course, the most important question in regard to these categories is the use to which they can be put. I suggest that these categories should enable us to understand the American student body more fully and plan more fully for their needs.

Each of these groups has had its quarrels with the

university but they are lovers' quarrels. They are bitter but they aim to change the university, not abolish it. Many of our Black and Puerto Rican students are hostile and angry because they have been unjustly kept out of the mainstream of American education and life for too long. Many still regard the university as a center of White oppression. But they want to come into the university, not to destroy it, but to use it. They see it as an avenue to success which has too long been closed to them, one which they wish to travel, not remove. So, too, the white lower-middle-class students. They ask the university to give them a wider view of the world than has been theirs in the past. They are willing to work hard at very traditional educational tasks.

There are other similarities and differences between these four groups of students in respect to the character of their preparation for college, their vocational aspirations, motivation, their needs for recreation and student services, their choice of curriculum, the character and extent of their participation in college governance and a host of other facets of their relationship to the university. It is almost as if the university were made up—and I quote Benjamin Disraeli's description of English class differences of more than a century ago—of separate "Nations," between whom "there is no intercourse and no sympathy"; nations "who are formed by different breeding, are fed by different food, are ordered by different manners and are not governed by the same laws."

But, of course, dwelling on the differences between these groups of our students tends to overstate the case, as does the suggestion—however forceful as a literary conceit—that they are separate nations, in Disraeli's terms. The differences must indeed be sought out, recognized and responded to. But we must also search out the similarities among our students, because it is only on the basis of these similarities that we can maintain a viable university, only on the basis of them that we can constitute a university community.

First and foremost among the things which bind American university students together is that they seek an education. They have come to the university to learn. And the significance of this common goal is tremendous. It causes all our students, however diverse they may otherwise be, to maintain a common ground on which the education they seek can be found. Moreover, an educational goal held in common virtually dictates a common attachment to certain educational values. The importance of experience as a tool of learning, the importance of objectivity, of scientific method, of literary and historical research, the importance, if you will, of just plain hard work; these educational values and many others as well are held in common among the most diverse of our students. Our diverse groups of students also share other, noneducational values. The right of an individual to be treated fairly, the right to privacy, the right of the individual to be his own master and achieve his own dignity, the right to express himself freely, the right to be free of coercion, free of bullies and tyrants and dictators—whatever other differences in their value systems there may be, I believe almost all American students share these values.

A common desire to seek an education, a common attachment to a set of educational values and a common belief in a set of political values—this is a broad enough and a firm enough base on which to maintain the strength and stability of a university. We should not, it seems to me, press for any more. We are not, after all, a commune or monastery and therefore we do not require nor would we be well served by all students' hewing to one ideology or to one vision of either the university or the world. The older university tradition suffered from just such homogeneity of purpose and people. Within broad limits, we should not only be able to tolerate difference, we should invite it and use it as an educational device. Diversity in its student body may make the life of the American university more difficult to manage, but it also makes the university a more challenging and more significant experience for its students and its faculty.

Ultimately, however, the success or failure of the

American university will turn on what students seek of the university, rather than what their social origins are. Students who come to us to learn the ways of knowing, to develop intellectual skills and to receive vocational and professional training can be well served. There are other motivations and aspirations, however, which simply cannot be served within the academic community as we know it. Let me examine some of these.

There are some students within the American university community who are "rip-off" artists. By a "rip-off" artist I mean someone who has thorough contempt for academic life and for society in general and who misuses his student status for the meanest kind of personal gain.

There is another group of students who come to the American university to seek status, rather than an education. Now it is indeed true that a university education confers status in our society and provides a passport of sorts to certain social preferments. But the fact is that the student who comes to the university seeking status, rather than an education, will probably gain neither. The only status the university can or should confer is the status of an education worked for and well-earned.

A third group of students comes to the university because there is no better place to go. Such students enroll because the draft threatens or because parents expect it of them, or because there is no ready employment or simply because it is the thing to do. The university is a kind of haven for these students, a haven from the life experience outside the university which they do not want to face.

A fourth group of American university students are acting out the role of social and political revolutionaries and are only incidentally working at being students. They look upon the university as a vantage point from which to force social change. They really disdain educational and intellectual values and are only interested in the university as a base of political operations.

Each of these students who enroll for the wrong reasons presents the university with a multitude of problems. They take up valuable space which could be better used by others. They lower the quality of work in the classrooms. They spread distrust and unease among their fellow students. They are a source of agitation against the legitimate exercise of university authority. And, finally, they bring the university and all its students into discredit in the eyes of the general public. Fortunately, these four groups of misfits constitute a rather small segment of American higher education; actually, the radical extremists and the "rip-off" artists represent a truly minuscule portion of the student body. My purpose—in speaking of them at all—is to disassociate them in the public mind from the overwhelming majority of our students.

As to that overwhelming majority of students, I am filled with hope. They are no older than students have traditionally been, but they have had much more experience of life. They come from homes and family backgrounds which have been less isolated from the centers of our economic and social life. The very style of family life in which they have been brought up is more open and honest, has made them more aware of what life is really about. And, finally, they show the effect of the communications revolution, for they reflect the influence of television and the film industry.

The sum of these influences has brought forth a generation of young people which is more sensitive to life in all its dimensions than any generation before. These young people have directly or vicariously experienced the whole range of human emotions and been witness to the whole play of political passions. Love and hatred; war, greed and bloodshed; discrimination, hunger and deprivation; electioneering and rioting: they have seen it all either directly or in ways which were not possible before the advent of the television tube.

The central task of the university during the next decade will be to confront a generation which has become cynical and despairing while still very young, which has rejected the life-style it inherited but which is still seeking its own. The university must somehow give this generation the courage and wit to do battle with the awesome injustices it inherits. War, racism, poverty and pollution are not discoveries the young have made on their own; they are the legacy we leave them. We must also provide them with the knowledge we have, so they may have at least a fighting chance to cope with these unholy gifts of our past and present.

The new student is seeking the tools for his task and life commitment in our universities. If we cannot provide them or if we are unwilling to provide them, they will not destroy us, they will just ignore us. If our world is to be remade into a humane place, it is going to be remade by the students in our universities today, acting intelligently and responsibly on the firm ground knowledge and reason provide. These students require an education which can serve as a lever of human reconstruction. We must respond by refashioning our university to serve the special character of our student body and their special purposes.

Parents of the Counterculture

A CULTURE IS a set of values, expectations, yearnings and fulfillments which are embodied in the way people earn their living, rear and educate their children, govern themselves, amuse themselves, love one another and otherwise go about their daily lives.

Going to school at an early age and continuing in education through our twenties to become teachers, or doctors, or housewives and mothers expresses a certain set of values. And so does saving money for the future, living in a suburb removed from our places of work, and finding sexual gratification exclusively in marriage.

The extraordinary fact which marks our days is that our children seem set upon rejecting our values.

Based upon an address delivered on August 24, 1971, before the National Convention of Hadassah, Cleveland, Ohio.

They seem to be going about their lives moved by a different set of compulsions, hopes, sources of joy and anticipation.

They are the children of a counterculture, building a new style of life, a new way of earning their living, a new way of finding love, playing, and governing themselves. This is the cultural revolution of our times; this is what the upheaval, uncertainty, anguish and joy of our youth is all about.

My thesis is a simple one: it is that the process of cultural upheaval we see going on around us is not really a children's crusade at all. To be sure, our children think they are the inventors of the counterculture; and the press, television, after-dinner speakers and other such pop-anthropologists support our children in this fallacy.

But our children and their popular chroniclers are mistaken. Cultural upheaval was in our wombs; we gave birth to the counterculture.

To be somewhat more precise: a cultural revolution is a vast change in the habits and life-style of a people. It is not to be confused with violent political upheaval. Cultural revolutions are really swelling tides of human feeling, expectation and belief called forth by profound, though subtle and elusive, changes in our social, economic, and ecological environment.

The distinctive role which our children play in the contemporary world is not that of instigators of social upheaval. They are rather bearing witness, openly and forcefully for all to see, of what has already happened; they are acting out a role which was already written before their birth, a role which we, their parents, prepared them for and coached them in. They have not originated change; they have only held up a mirror to the change which was already taking place when they were born.

We are at the end of a period of development which began with the introduction of the factory and culminated in the development of electronic communications systems and the computer, a period of industrialization, of mass communication, and of automation. Supporting these changes, providing them with necessary intellectual tools, motive force and moral justification was a profound attachment to reason and scientific method and an equally profound commitment to a religious ethic based on salvation through discipline, forbearance and mastery of nature. Changes in the way man gained his sustenance and produced his goods were, of course, reflected in the corresponding changes in the homes men established for their families and in the way they nurtured their children. The home as a center of work, whether a farm home or a home in which products were produced for market, was first transformed into a home near a place of work. It was still influenced, however, by the mood, rhythms, and discipline of work. It was then transformed into a suburban home, a home intentionally isolated from the world of work.

As this was happening, the home was also being supplanted as a center of nurture and education. The parent was replaced as a teacher by a class of professional teachers and then by the appearance of those new educational tools—radio, television, films, and other mass media. Schools and universities began to grow in size and to remove themselves, both physically and emotionally, from the life of the home. As industry and the social and political organizations which supported it grew in size and complexity, they demanded more educated and sophisticated workers and managers. Training for such roles required ever longer periods of time, so that the normal span of education grew from a few short years to, at the extreme, twenty to twenty-five years.

Man's very success in the conquest of nature and the production of goods, and the social and economic organization which made that possible were themselves potent influences in changing the character of his life. The search for material goods and worldly possessions began to dominate man's consciousness. Securing a position of strength and status in society began to supplant all other goals and values. The attainment of wealth and status became a secular religion, a form of worldly salvation. Science and rationality, organization and technological control, money and goods—these became gods for men to worship rather than tools for men to use.

In our own century, the voices of social criticism have grown increasingly loud as the evidence of the depredation wreaked by our material successes has become ever more clear. Cycles of economic depression, colonial exploitation, racial discrimination, the impoverishment of a large segment of our population, recurrent wars and the threat of a nuclear holocaust, the use of mass social organization and state power in totalitarian countries to throttle individual liberty, the poisoning of our air and water by industrial wastes—these and a myriad other such ills began to shake our confidence in our social and economic structure.

What we began to see in suburbia led to a similar disillusionment with family life: homes filled with goods, but low on love; rates of divorce, promiscuity, and alcoholism rising steeply; wives who had achieved the status of social matrons, but were bored and felt useless and unloved; successful husbands, who were overworked and driven with anxiety by the unrelenting demands of the technological machine; children living at home, but actually being nurtured by their peers, by baby-sitters and by omnipresent television sets and, therefore, feeling unwanted and unloved.

The children of the counterculture, however, are not a homogeneous bunch. They are actually bound together by little more than their common disdain

for established ways. They are political revolutionaries and gradualists, and there are even some solid
political conservatives among them. They are loners
and communalists. They are drug-users, drunks, and
abstainers. They are hip and they are square. They
are sexually promiscuous and sexually pure. They are
aggressive and they are passive. They run, in fact, a
wide range of personality types and behavior patterns.
What binds our youth together is, as Paul Goodman
has remarked, that they are protestants seeking a new
reformation. They say, as Luther said before them,
"God has turned his face away, things have no mean-
ing, I am estranged in the world."

You and I, middle-class parents, must face a colos-
sal irony: Why is it our children who feel dispos-
sessed? Why do our best-educated youngsters, with
easy access to any and all of our social privileges and
rewards, feel like strangers in our culture? The reason
our middle-class children lack cultural roots and feel
alienated is that they mirror the insecurity of our
own lives, they reflect our own skepticism about the
world they will soon inherit from us.

But then, you will ask, why are they any different
from us?

We were the children of poverty who came into
affluence. We knew the relationship between disciplined effort and reward. We knew what wanting,
doing without and waiting was like. They have lived

with affluence all their lives and have not learned to want, to wait for or to work for what they enjoy.

We grew up in a world where we were still able to watch our fathers at work and we saw the fruit their labors bore. Their fathers work in a world removed, at tasks so technologically complex and so deeply embedded in an organizational structure that the link between effort and result is obscured.

We grew up with mothers who toiled at housework and took pride, if not joy, in their labor. They grow up not with homemakers, but with managers of homes filled with appliances, with mothers who are increasingly estranged and in flight from their roles.

We grew up in a world where we occasionally played with friends, but we lived with our parents, feeling their influence deeply even when their work forced them to be away from us. They grow up in a world where friends have become more important than parents and where parents are not at home even when they are at home.

We grew up in a world where our parents said no, even when they had some doubt about what was right and wrong. And, our parents disciplined us as an act of their love. They grow up in a world in which moral skepticism has turned parents into ethical eunuchs, referees rather than sources of direction, and where punishment is taken to be an act of denial instead of an act of caring.

We grew up in a world in which our sexual and social maturity coincided with the completion of our education and, during the relatively short term of our education, we could look forward eagerly to working productively at what we had learned. They grow up in a world in which they mature at a much earlier age than we did, but are educated in the ways of our advanced technology for a much longer time. They are ready for life long before it is ready for them. They seem to be waiting an interminable period to go to work at tasks they do not relish.

We learned our lessons as children from books and from teachers who themselves loved books. What we learned took time to learn; learning was an experience requiring effort. They learn some of their most potent lessons on television, where learning is a dramatic event, something which is selected for them and not an experience in which they participate and at which they work.

War, racial discrimination and sexual perversion were not part of our daily fare as youngsters. We learned about depravity slowly, as we matured, and only by dint of a voluntary effort to read daily newspapers and books. Through television, our children are involuntarily inundated with the cruelty and inhumanity of life before they have developed the emotional or intellectual perspective to cope with it.

We grew up in a world in which the natural rhythms of the days and seasons still largely determined the tempo of our lives and in which the air was fresh to breathe and flowers were sweet to smell. They grow up with pocket parks, amidst the constant unnerving roar of automobiles and jet planes. They feel as if they were engulfed in the stench and unsightliness of our industrial and personal waste.

We grew up with benign and legitimate authority figures as well as irresponsible and malevolent ones. We had experience of just wars and unjust ones, emotionally fulfilling patriotism and irrational, destructive chauvinism. They have never learned to love any figure of authority, whether in the home or the nation. And, the one war they know at first hand has so filled their lives with its inhumanity that it has turned patriotism into a bad word and love of country into a vanishing emotion.

Finally, we grew up in a world which was still uncrowded and in which the pall of an atomic holocaust was as yet unknown. We could look forward to having children, to nourishing them and enduring in and through them. For our children, the pressure of an exploding world population and the ever present threat of nuclear obliteration has attached guilt and foreboding to the maternal instinct.

These then, are some of the reasons why our children have such a different response to our way of life, why they are a counterculture. We expose them with a brutal honesty to our failures, without providing them with the emotional stability, the moral direction or discipline, and the intellectual perspective necessary to correct them. We brought them into a world blighted by poverty, racial injustice, war, over-population and pollution, without providing them with the redeeming faith, optimism and courage to persevere into the future.

We transmitted to them our own disillusion with the worship of reason, science, and technology, without an adequate understanding on their part, or ours for that matter, of the appropriate role these cultural tools must necessarily play in the life of man. Our children bear all our scars and mirror all our anxieties, without the benefit of our strengths, without our attachment to life and without our intellectual heritage.

As a consequence, children of the counterculture seek a new life, a life of love, beauty and simplicity in which they can search out the unique joy and agony of their existence. They want to take a journey inward, they want to liberate consciousness and enhance the quality of their subjective experience.

They would replace our materialism with a new attachment to the human spirit, supplant our devotion to science and reason with a commitment to intuition, imagination, and sensation; be moved by impulse, desire and choice, rather than order and regulation; live and work as individuals or in extended friendship or family groups, rather than as isolated nuclear families or units in mass organizations; give up competition and status for love and the satisfaction of just being.

But just as we and our children judge ourselves by what we do rather than by what we profess, so must we judge our children. As we have seen, they profess individuality but exemplify conformity in their attachment to their own hair styles and dress codes. They profess humanism, but they tend to degrade reason, the very quality which makes us human. They seek joy in sexuality in the midst of multitudes. They celebrate consciousness, but then paralyze it with drugs. They eschew our technology, but delight in motor bikes, electronic music, recordings, television, and hi-fi. They thoroughly disdain wealth and property, but live, often in high style (and guilt-ridden, to be sure), on parental allowances. They profess to the love of all mankind, but many of them steal and cheat from each other and from us. They seek universal peace, but often undertake or applaud violence in the service of their ends. They pretend to humility, but display arrogance and self-righteousness towards those with whom they disagree. They cherish the freedom to express themselves, but would often deny that right to those they violently oppose.

Thus, our children, no less than we, are failing themselves. They are caught in a web of contradiction and hypocrisy.

The generation gap is a dangerous myth which creates a barrier between us and our children. To be sure, I am my child's father, not her brother. We have different ranges of responsibility, energy, experience, knowledge and sensitivity. There are many things we cannot, and should not, share. We do, however, share a sense of the imperfection of our society, and a common sense of human frailty, of having our ideals thwarted and compromised, and a feeling that the quality of life must now be placed at the center of man's agenda. Our children did not invent social protest and they did not initiate the search for a counterculture. These were part of their inheritance from us, it is an inheritance which we share.

We must, therefore, join them, not fight them. We must wed our maturity to their energy, our knowledge to their imagination, our technology to their motivation, our political sophistication to their moral intuition—and together we shall overcome.

Part III
Governing the Contemporary University

A New Academic Social Contract

THE EROSION OF established authority is the fundamental fact of life on college campuses today, evidenced by the erosion of the academic order in the kinds of questions which are searching for answers. How shall a college president be chosen? How shall faculty be appointed and reappointed? How shall a curriculum be established and changed? How shall new academic buildings be planned? How shall standards of academic achievement be measured? How shall student social life be regulated? As we have seen, there was a time when each of these procedural questions and hundreds of others like them had a ready answer, most frequently implicit.

As we college presidents know by dint of our daily

Presidential Forum Address delivered on January 12, 1970, at the Annual Meeting of the Association of American Colleges, Houston, Texas.

pain and perplexity, this is no longer true. The time is out of joint and the whole machinery of the college has come unhinged. Administering a college today is like playing chess on the open deck of the sinking *Titanic*—to make matters worse, the chess rules seem to be changing as the game proceeds.

The image of the Hobbesian state of nature may be somewhat overblown as applied to our college campuses. But many of us do indeed suffer continual fear and danger of violent confrontation, and the life of academic man has become poorer, nastier and somewhat more brutish and short on its rewards.

Suspicion and distrust have begun to work in corrosive influence in the groves of academe. Lost is the sense of community, the sense of what made us one with one another. In its place there is found estrangement and sectarianism.

A primary consequence of the erosion of the academic order is that we feel less free to say and do what we want. A new spirit of intimidation has been born on our campuses and it is fed from two sides. On the one side, some college presidents answer any and all challenges to the established order as if a gun had been drawn to their heads; they make too ready use of academic and civil disciplinary forces. On the other side, some students and faculty have sought to impose their views by calling upon the force of student numbers and passions. A student body aroused to an emotional pitch is no great respecter of dissent.

It can be as potent a source of the suppression of freedom as cop's clubs or court orders.

Why is our academic order eroding and why is the politics of coercion and intimidation spreading from one campus to another? The academic social contract no longer stands intact because, as we have seen, our young have lost faith in us and in the institutions, social and academic, which we represent. They no longer believe in us or admire us; in many instances, they don't even like us. We neither share their mood nor their manner. We symbolize for them an order which has failed them, a decadent social order which feeds on war, poverty, racial injustice and despoliation of our natural environment and resources, while glorying in vulgar materialism.

Many mistaken responses to the turmoil about us are being urged. On the one side, there are those who tell us that all we academic administrators need is a firm hand with the unruly few. This reminds me of Tzar Nicholas' response to the Petrograd riots of March, 1918. "Bring in another company of troops," he said. He should have known, as we must know, that "a King is not saved by his great army, a warrior is not delivered by his great strength." Moreover, once the academic order becomes an order of force it contradicts its essential nature.

And then there are those who tell us that all academic change must be orderly and lawful; that if we once admit or admire any use of illegal or coercive tactics we open the way to tyranny. But who would deny that some institutions can only be changed by shock and disruption? Who would deny that some systems of order work to thwart change and preserve inequities and injustices? An orderly process is not necessarily a politically neutral process, nor is an orderly process necessarily a just process. It may well be that the student upheaval of the 1960's will be remembered with the sit-in strikes and mortgage burnings of the 1930's as necessary incidents in the progressive development of American life.

On the other side, there are those who argue that force and obstruction alone can change academic institutions. They argue that all academic process is necessarily corrupt and represents an insuperable obstacle to academic renewal. The answer to these critics of peaceable change is that they are not sufficiently discriminating. Some institutions are capable of radical change by dint of reasonable argument and without intimidation or disruption; others are not. Failure to make this distinction is a symptom of ideological blindness.

Opponents of the established academic order also urge that the use of any force from outside the institution violates its very spirit. This argument must be granted, except we should note that it comes with little grace and with even less honesty in the mouths of those who have themselves been guilty of invoking force on the college campus. The defenseless institution must defend itself against those who would disrupt it without good cause. The blame in such instances lies not with those administrators who undertake the use of force in defense of the institution, but rather with those who have initiated the use of force in the first instance.

Thus, this is neither the time for unyielding maintenance of academic order nor for changes in that order carried out by dint of intimidation and disruption. What our times call for is a new and for the most part peaceable accommodation of those diverse interests which make up the academic community. It requires a new academic social contract, a new set of shared assumptions about the nature and purposes of the educational community. To paraphrase Rousseau: We must find some form of association as a result of which the whole strength of the academic community will be enlisted for the protection of the right of each constituent in it to teach and study in such a way that each, when united with his fellows renders obedience to his own will and remains as free as he was before.

A new social contract does not come into being with the signing of a document. It does not arise out of a constituent assembly, nor is it the product of rational agreement. It is rather the outcome of a process of organic growth, a process which is taking place now amidst the shattering of the old academic order. Its main tendencies are there for all of us to see. Let me attempt to sketch them:

We begin with the recognition that there is no single immutable Platonic idea of the university to be held in trust for all time by guardians of its purity. The university and college of today are called upon to serve changing and diverse interests of changing and diverse men. Moreover, these interests are not capable of being demonstrably or conclusively established by trustees of an ideal, but must be accommodated one to another in a political process. That is, the varied interests brought together in the college or university must compete with one another for recognition, and in such a process of competition the institution will constantly remake and revitalize itself.

A second condition for the growth of a new academic social contract is to free academic administrators from a commitment to prevailing national and community values. Unless administrators are free to oppose an unjust war, to militate against archaic conventional mores, to attack social injustice, unless administrators are able to take such stands, they cannot maintain the trust and allegiance of their academic constituency.

I do not advocate that the university or college itself should become institutionally committed to political or moral positions. I urge, rather, that college presidents be free to speak their minds on the great issues of the day. The institution's neutrality on such issues is vital and should not under any circumstances be sacrificed. But the administrator's neutrality on such issues leaves him open to the charge of hypocrisy or, worse yet, the charge of being morally and politically wed to the status quo.

Next, the academic community will require new, more representative leaders. Today's university and college presidents are constitutionally illegitimate. They are chosen by and are only accountable to the wider community acting through a board of trustees. This leaves the college president without a constitutional tie to either the faculty or the student body. His authority, his moral claim to leadership, is diminished by the very narrow base of his accountability. Leaders of the new academic order must be expressive of the common will embodied in that order. They must, therefore, be truly representative of all its constituent interests and elements, including its faculty and student body.

A fourth condition for the growth of the new academic community is the recognition that academic egalitarianism is a mechanical and simplistic response to the question, who shall govern the college. People come together in a college or university for a special purpose, and that purpose, rather than the purpose for which political communities exist, should define the role which each member of the community plays in it. "One man, one vote" makes sense in a community in which every man has the same right to life, liberty and happiness and in which the preservation of that right constitutes the very reason for the community's existence. This egalitarian principle makes no sense, however, in a limited-purpose community into which classes of individuals enter for different reasons and bring to it different skills and interests which relate differently to its aims.

Although on occasion students teach each other and learn on their own, they come to a college or university for the primary purpose of learning from members of the faculty. Moreover, students not only enter the academic community for a limited purpose, they also enter it for a limited time. Faculty, however, enter the academic community with a different purpose; they enter to teach and to engage in scholarly, artistic and scientific pursuits. Moreover, they enter the community for extended periods of time, frequently as a life work. Finally, trustees, representatives of the wider community who are not themselves resident in the academic community and neither teach nor learn in it, participate in it in order to assure that it serves the community's purposes.

The very description of each of these functional roles and its relationship to the aims of academe supports the conclusion that each constituency of the university community has a different claim of right in respect of its governance. The claim of right of each must be founded on and be appropriate to the specific competence and interest which it brings to the institution's special purpose.

Alfred North Whitehead stated the case in philosophic terms: "The tragedy of the world is that those who are imaginative have but slight experience, and those who are experienced have feeble imaginations. Fools act on imagination without knowledge; pedants act on knowledge without imagination. The task of a university is to weld together imagination and experience." I urge that the development of the new academic social contract requires a recognition of the appropriate sphere of imagination and experience and requires that each receive due but different acknowledgment in the governance of the community.

Next we require academic leadership which can maintain emotional, cultural and ethical identification with the student body. The day of the college president as a benign father-figure is over. The day of the college president as a wise faculty-member-turned-administrator is also over. We now need a college president who is not only politically accountable to students, but also one who understands them well enough to speak in their name, to represent them.

We need not, and should not, replace the paternal with the fraternal president. We must, however, replace the president who "knows what's best for students" with one who responds to what students themselves think is best for themselves. This is not to say that the college president must agree with his students in order to represent them. It is to say that the college president must understand his students in order to represent them, and he must represent them as they understand themselves rather than as he would have them understand themselves. In sum, the college president can no longer be a force alien to the student body.

A final precondition for the creation of a new academic order is that our society begin to devote sufficient resources to higher education. In some large measure, the contemporary crisis of academic authority is a response to the fact that the academic community has had totally inadequate resources to meet its burgeoning needs. No system of authority can long stand the test of failing to meet the essential needs of its constituents. To be sure, political leadership always involves denying resources to some and awarding them to others. The special difficulty of many colleges and universities today is that educational needs have so far outstripped capacity that they can no longer pretend to fulfill their educational function. A starving society cannot long maintain political stability, nor can a starved educational system. A new political synthesis in the college and university awaits the commitment of a fuller share of the national budget to higher education.

A sense of the college and university as defining its goals through a process of political accommodation of the conflicting wishes of its varied constituencies; a college president representative of the full range of interests embodied in the institution; a president freed from commitment to dominant social, political and moral values and capable of personal and emotional identification with his student constituents; a structure of governance which admits students, faculty and trustees into political participation, but defines the role of each in terms of its special interests and competencies; and resources sufficient to meet basic needs: these are the grounds on which a new academic social contract can flourish. These are the grounds which can help to restore the bonds of sympathy and admiration, the shared expectations, hopes, fears and faith which support the exercise of authority. These are the grounds which can restore academic order and insure academic freedom by legitimating academic authority.

The Constitutional Crisis in Academia

THE TRADITIONAL COLLEGE pursued its goals with vitality, internal harmony and a clear sense of purpose. It was organized like a business corporation. A relatively small board of trustees—the counterpart of the corporate board of directors—exercised complete dominion over the college. This board delegated full operating authority to a college president, and he served at the board's will, responsible to them and them alone. The faculty was chosen by the president and was responsible to him much as employees are to a corporate president. And the student body enjoyed a status somewhat between that of a customer of an educational product and that of a ward of an educational guardian.

Inaugural Convocation Address delivered on November 12, 1971, in the First Presbyterian Church, Camden, New Jersey.

110

The day has long passed since this model of academic governance found sanction in custom, effectiveness and the common sense of legitimacy. Yet the model persists, enshrined in state laws, academic statutes and the popular consciousness. The discrepancy between an ineffectual governing structure and the requirement that complex universities be ordered by a sense of common purpose and direction underlies most of what has troubled academic life in the recent past. We have been in a constitutional crisis.

A structure of authority is a delicate thing. Force and implicit threats of force, although often identified as of the very essence of government, are really only its most obvious attributes and are hardly sufficient to sustain it. As Rousseau said in the *Social Contract:* "The strongest man is never strong enough unless he transforms his power into right and obedience into duty." Acquiescence, habitual obedience, intuitive responsiveness to felt need and an aura of moral fitness must all contribute their saving grace to transmute force into sustained and legitimate authority.

To be sure, we cannot attribute all of the recent tensions on our campuses to an anachronistic governing structure. Nor can we suppose that a recent diminution of the disorder in academia is exclusively a result of changes in governance. But the evolution of a new instrument of governance has surely helped —to use Rousseau's terms once more—to transform academic "power into right and obedience into duty." The process of restructuring is not yet completed in this university or in others. But the main outlines have become clear. To understand them, however, it may be best to look at the four differing governing models which have been vying for ascendancy in the university in recent years. Since the role of the university president was central to the traditional governing scheme, it is not surprising to find that the conception of that role is a key feature which distinguishes the four models. For convenience then, let me refer to the four academic-governance models in terms which reflect the varying political positions of the university president.

The university with a "Responsive President": The underlying supposition of this model is that the only thing wrong with the traditional structure of governance was that it failed to "communicate" with and was not sufficiently "responsive" to the values and consciousness of faculty and students. The solution which is proposed in this model is to create numerous new committees of trustees, administration, faculty, students and alumni, which committees would serve to foster "communication" and to make the traditional authoritarian hierarchy "responsive." The weakness of this proposal is that it mistakes the real basis of the academic crisis of legitimacy. What has been at issue fundamentally is not that the governing body is unresponsive, but rather that the

governing body as it has been traditionally consti-
tuted has no moral right to exercise ultimate and
exclusive governing authority. Committees which are
heard but need never be heeded may well help maintain the responsiveness of an authoritarian leader.
But responsive or benevolent authority is not to be
confused with responsible or accountable authority.
In the long run, no institution can remain sufficiently
responsive to those it serves, however well-intentioned and however well-managed, unless it is accountable to them.

The university with a "Custodial President":
There are some who feel academia suffers from the
same malady from which government generally suffers. The problem, they feel, is that any bureaucracy,
any governing body, no matter how it is chosen or
sanctioned, really never serves any interest but its
own. The solution proposed in this model is to do
away with all political leadership and allow those
affected to fashion directly the decisions which affect
them. In such a participatory system of governance,
there would be no need for trustees and the university president would make no decisions. He would
merely see that the floors were clean and that other
such chores were done efficiently.

I confess that this vision of governance has great
appeal to me, especially in a day when so many of
our bureaucracies seem to have done such a poor job
of governing. Its appeal is to the strong urge we all

have to be our own masters in all things. Its weakness is that none of us have the time, or the skill and knowledge to function as our own masters. That is why direct democracy only works, when it does at all, in respect to a very limited number of issues and with small groups of people. Most often it is simply too time-consuming, too inefficient and too ineffectual, and often it becomes a facade behind which elites operate most irresponsibly. Actually, many colleges and universities have recently operated with a modified form of the "Custodial President" model of governance. Sensitive to challenges to their authority, many presidents have delegated much of their decision-making to committees of faculty and students. If there are enough committees and if they are representative enough, and if the delegating authority rarely exercises any control over them, the result is indeed a form of participatory democracy. There is no doubt but that some calm has been obtained on some campuses by such decentralization of authority. But the price paid for it has been heavy. The university has been left without central direction; the system involves extraordinary expenditures of student and faculty energy; and the process of decentralization tends to enshrine the status quo in higher education.

All of which is not to say that universities can or should be governed without committees; it is only to say that a structure of such committees is not an adequate substitute for a university president or an executive authority.

The college with a "Faculty President": John Kenneth Galbraith and McGeorge Bundy, each in his own way, have suggested that the faculty could constitute the sovereign source of academic authority in place of a board of trustees. Such a faculty would elect a president who would serve at its pleasure rather than at the pleasure of the board of trustees. Again, this seems like an appealing solution. But it has incurable weaknesses. There are strong faculty interests, the interest in high salaries for one, which tend to pose a conflict with student, alumni and public interests. Moreover, a president subject solely to the pleasure of the faculty would be too subject to the ephemeral turns of faculty sentiment to provide stable and sustained leadership. Finally, the faculty simply do not have the management, financial and community relations skills and sensibilities which boards of trustees exercise to such great advantage.

The university with a "Constitutional President": This is the model we come closest to at Rutgers today. I believe it is also the model which in the long run will promise most success as an instrument of sound, efficient and responsible academic governance. The traditional "trustee president" system eroded because the president's mandate was derived exclusively from a relatively small body of trustees who represented only a limited set of the interests in the uni-

versity—those of the general public. The substitution
of a "Responsive President" is a step forward but it
does not address itself to the heart of the constitutional distress, the moral basis of the president's authority. A "Custodial President" system, in its extreme form is either utopian or a fraud; in its less
extreme form of governance by representative committees it is weak, indecisive and ineffectual. A "Faculty President" system promises to be unstable, un-
settling to the faculty and unrepresentative of the
interests of students, alumni and the community at
large.

The only alternative which seems to be viable is
to create a new central university authority which is
responsible to a new and legitimate source of academic sovereignty, one truly representative of the
entire range of academic interests. This new source
of authority should be accountable and responsive to
the claims of faculty, students, alumni and the public
at large, as represented by a board of trustees. Such
a community requires, not a guardian or trustee, but
a constitutional mechanism for giving expression to
and finding mutual accommodation between the
variety of purposes and goals the academic community embodies. Students, faculty, alumni and the public at large all have a moral claim on the operation
of a university. That claim or interest can only be
protected appropriately if the president of the uni-

versity is in some measure accountable for his stewardship to each of those constituencies.

Such a "constitutional presidency" overcomes the academic crisis of legitimacy by providing the president with a new and broader mandate which serves to legitimize him. It also gives the president authority commensurate with his responsibility and thereby helps to assure vital and purposive direction to the academic community. To be sure, the best political solutions are found in the hearts and sentiments of men rather than in legal and constitutional forms. But sometimes a change in the hearts and sentiments of men is made possible when legal forms which were found to be inequitable and ineffectual are abandoned for new ones.

ABOUT THE AUTHOR

Dr. Bloustein received a Bachelor of Philosophy degree from Oxford University, which he had attended as a Fulbright Scholar, and a Ph.D. and a law degree from Cornell University. He has taught philosophy both at Brooklyn College and Cornell and law at New York University. He served as a political analyst for the State Department in 1951–52 and again in 1955–56 and as a law clerk in the New York State Court of Appeals from 1965 to 1971. He was inaugurated as the seventeenth president of Rutgers University, the State University of New Jersey in November 1971.

Dr. Bloustein is author or coauthor of a number of monographs published in law reviews and journals; of two studies for the State Department; of *Dimensions of Academic Freedom* (1969), with others; of *Due Process; Report and Recommendations on Admission to Mental Hospitals under New York Law* (1962); and he is editor of *Nuclear Energy, Public Policy, and the Law* (1964).

The text of this book was set in Baskerville Linotype and printed by Offset on P & S Special Book manufactured by P. H. Glatfelter Co., Spring Grove, Pa. Composed, printed and bound by Quinn & Boden Company, Inc., Rahway, N.J.